Business Simulations, Games and Experiential Learning in International Business Education

Business Simulations, Games and Experiential Learning in International Business Education

Joseph Wolfe, PhD
J. Bernard Keys, PhD
Editors

International Business Press
An Imprint of
The Haworth Press, Inc.
New York • London

Published by

International Business Press, 10 Alice Street, Binghamton, NY 13904-1580 USA

International Business Press is an imprint of The Haworth Press, Inc., 10 Alice Street, Binghamton, NY 13904-1580 USA.

Business Simulations, Games and Experiential Learning in International Business Education has also been published as *Journal of Teaching in International Business*, Volume 8, Number 4 1997.

Library of Congress Cataloging-in-Publication Data

Business simulations, games and experiential learning in international business education/Joseph Wolfe, J. Bernard Keys, editors.
    p. cm.
    Includes bibliographical references and index.
    ISBN 0-7890-0041-5 (alk. paper).–ISBN 0-7890-0309-0 (alk. paper)
    1. Business education–Simulation methods. 2. Management–Study and teaching–Simulation methods. I. Wolfe, Joseph. II. Keys, J. Bernard.
HF1106.B945 1997
650′.071′5–dc21
                                                                   97-758
                                                                                 CIP

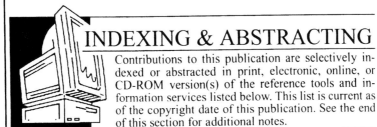

INDEXING & ABSTRACTING

Contributions to this publication are selectively indexed or abstracted in print, electronic, online, or CD-ROM version(s) of the reference tools and information services listed below. This list is current as of the copyright date of this publication. See the end of this section for additional notes.

- ***Business Education Index, The***, Eastern Illinois University, Department of Business Education and Administration Information Systems, Charleston, IL 61920

- ***CNPIEC Reference Guide: Chinese National Directory of Foreign Periodicals***, P.O. Box 88, Beijing, People's Republic of China

- ***Contents Pages in Education***, Carfax Information Systems, P.O. Box 25, Abingdon, Oxfordshire OX14 3UE, United Kingdom

- ***Contents Pages in Management***, University of Manchester Business School, Booth Street West, Manchester M15 6PB, England

- ***Educational Technology Abstracts***, Carfax Publishing Company, P.O. Box 25, Abingdon, Oxfordshire OX14 3UE, United Kingdom

- ***IBZ International Bibliography of Periodical Literature***, Zeller Verlag GmbH & Co., P.O.B. 1949, D-49009 Osnabruck, Germany

- ***Index to Periodical Articles Related to Law***, University of Texas, 727 East 26th Street, Austin, TX 78705

- ***International Bulletin of Bibliography on Education***, Proyecto B.I.B.E./Apartado 52, San Lorenzo del Escorial, Madrid, Spain

(continued)

- *INTERNET ACCESS (& additional networks) Bulletin Board for Libraries ("BUBL"), coverage of information resources on INTERNET, JANET, and other networks.*
  - JANET X.29: UK.AC.BATH.BUBL or 00006012101300
  - TELNET: BUBL.BATH.AC.UK or 138.38.32.45 login 'bubl'
  - Gopher: BUBL.BATH.AC.UK (138.32.32.45). Port 7070
  - World Wide Web: http: / / www.bubl.bath.ac.uk./BUBL/ home.html
  - NISSWAIS: telnetniss.ac.uk (for the NISS gateway)
  The Andersonian Library, Curran Building, 101 St. James Road, Glasgow G4 0NS, Scotland

- *Journal of Abstracts in International Education*, Two The Oaks Drive, Ashland, KY 41101

- *Journal of Health Care Marketing (abstracts section)*, Georgia Tech-School of Management, Ivan Allen College, 225 North Avenue NW, Atlanta, GA 30332

- *Linguistics and Language Behavior Abstracts (LLBA)*, Sociological Abstracts, Inc., P.O. Box 22206, San Diego, CA 92192-0206

- *Management & Marketing Abstracts*, Pira International, Randalls Road, Leatherhead, Surrey KT22 7RU, England

- *Medication Use STudies (MUST) DATABASE*, The University of Mississippi, School of Pharmacy, University, MS 38677

- *Resources in Education (RIE)*, George Washington University, One Depot Circle, Suite 630, Washington, DC 20036-1183

- *Social Planning/Policy & Development Abstracts (SOPODA)*, Sociological Abstracts, Inc., P.O. Box 22206, San Diego, CA 92192-0206

- *Sociological Abstracts (SA)*, Sociological Abstracts, Inc., P.O. Box 22206, San Diego, CA 92192-0206

- *Technical Education & Training Abstracts*, Carfax Publishing Company, P.O. Box 25, Abingdon, Oxfordshire OX14 3UE, United Kingdom

(continued)

SPECIAL BIBLIOGRAPHIC NOTES

related to special journal issues (separates)
and indexing/abstracting

☐ indexing/abstracting services in this list will also cover material in any "separate" that is co-published simultaneously with Haworth's special thematic journal issue or DocuSerial. Indexing/abstracting usually covers material at the article/chapter level.

☐ monographic co-editions are intended for either non-subscribers or libraries which intend to purchase a second copy for their circulating collections.

☐ monographic co-editions are reported to all jobbers/wholesalers/approval plans. The source journal is listed as the "series" to assist the prevention of duplicate purchasing in the same manner utilized for books-in-series.

☐ to facilitate user/access services all indexing/abstracting services are encouraged to utilize the co-indexing entry note indicated at the bottom of the first page of each article/chapter/contribution.

☐ this is intended to assist a library user of any reference tool (whether print, electronic, online, or CD-ROM) to locate the monographic version if the library has purchased this version but not a subscription to the source journal.

☐ individual articles/chapters in any Haworth publication are also available through the Haworth Document Delivery Services (HDDS).

Business Simulations, Games and Experiential Learning in International Business Education

CONTENTS

ABOUT THE EDITORS

Joseph Wolfe, PhD, is Professor of Management in the College of Business Administration at the University of Tulsa. He has actively researched and practiced in the area of experiential learning methods in both their business gaming and case research forms. In recent years, he has spent much time bringing experiential learning techniques to Poland, Hungary, Russia, and the Ukraine. Dr. Wolfe has served as a Fulbright Lecturer in Strategic Management at Hungary's International Management Center in Budapest, the former Eastern bloc's first private MBA program, and has conducted case research studies on two of Hungary's largest enterprises, the Csepel Machine Tool Works and the Taurus Hungarian Rubber Company. A past President of the Association of Business Simulation and Experiential Learning and past Chair of the Academy of Management's Management Education and Development Division, Dr. Wolfe is a member of the editorial boards of *Simulation & Gaming, Management Learning*, and the *Case Research Journal*.

J. Bernard Keys, PhD, is Fuller E. Callaway Professor and Director of the Center for Managerial Learning and Business Simulation at Georgia Southern University in Stateboro. The former Associate Dean for Graduate Programs at The University of Memphis, he recently served as Erskine Fellow at the University of Canterbury in New Zealand. He is currently a consultant to ELEA, Olivetta Learning Consultancy in Florence, Italy. Dr. Keys has been the Editor of *Executive Development* and *The Journal of Management Development*, as well as Associate Editor of the *Journal of Simulation and Gaming*. The Co-Author of *The Multinational Management Game* (Microbusiness Publications), a book now in its fourth edition, he is presently editing a book called *Executive Development and Organizational Learning for a Global World* (International Business Press). He is a past President of the Southern Management Association and of the International Management Development Association, as well as the founding President of the Association for Business Simulation and Experiential Learning. He is a Fellow in the International Academy of Management.

Introduction

Joseph Wolfe

J. Bernard Keys

Numerous business practitioners and educators have opined that traditional management education and development methods will not suffice when training managers for the global environments in which they will compete. Managers in our global economy must deal with cultural diversity and different perspectives and values, attempt to apply "home grown" technologies to foreign situations while negotiating the technologies and knowledges possessed by those in host nations, be linguistically flexible and accomplish their tasks in shifting economic circumstances. Accordingly, it is reasoned that the teaching methods used to train and develop these managers must possess qualities that challenge and alter their belief systems, promote decision making and management style flexibility while insuring that the business rules and regulations found in particular countries are understood and can be applied accurately.

While this is a tall educational order, business games, simulations and cases, used both singly and in combination, have the power to bring about such results. Taken as a group, these experiential or active learning teaching technologies place learners into fairly realistic yet psychologically-safe learning situations where they can experiment with new behaviors with immediate, constructive feedback. Within these environments old psycho-cultural assumptions can be challenged, perspectives can be broadened

---

Joseph Wolfe is Professor of Management at the University of Tulsa. J. Bernard Keys is Fuller E. Callaway Professor of Business at the Center for Managerial Learning and Business Simulation, Georgia Southern University.

[Haworth co-indexing entry note]: "Introduction." Wolfe, Joseph, and J. Bernard Keys. Co-published simultaneously in *Journal of Teaching in International Business* (International Business Press, an imprint of The Haworth Press, Inc.) Vol. 8, No. 4, 1997, pp. 1-3; and: *Business Simulations, Games and Experiential Learning in International Business Education* (ed: Joseph Wolfe, and J. Bernard Keys) International Business Press, an imprint of The Haworth Press, Inc., 1997, pp. 1-3. Single or multiple copies of this article are available for a fee from The Haworth Document Delivery Service [1-800-342-9678, 9:00 a.m. - 5:00 p.m. (EST). E-mail address: getinfo@haworth.com].

and critical reflection is stimulated. While traditional lectures "can get out the facts" and provoke an enthusiastic response and a good video presentation can exemplify and summarize a particular situation and its accompanying dilemmas, experiential techniques go more to the "soul" of the individual while also insuring a greater amount of learning transfer to the job situation.

A vast literature has been accumulated over the years regarding the management education and development techniques available and their effects (Wexley and Baldwin, 1986; Keys and Wolfe, 1988). This volume deals with the application and usefulness of various experiential technologies for the education of managers in the international sphere. While summary reviews of the general experiential literature are available (Keys and Wolfe, 1990; Gosenpud, 1990; Wolfe, 1990), the five articles in this volume present applications that have addressed the unique educational requirements of the global manager and those who aspire to these positions. In the first article, Kevin W. Boyack and Marshall Berman describe what could be considered an "ice-breaking" game designed to introduce MBA students to global competition and business cultures while exploring the ethical, political and social issues associated with this context. First-year MBAs engage in a free-form, role-based game where they play American and Japanese business roles while making strategy decisions and reflecting on their processes and outcomes.

Jeremiah J. O'Connell has developed a cultural simulation to teach the subtleties of the strong preference Europeans have toward participation and involvement in their society and workplace. Again in an MBA setting, students role-play the members of a European works council and experience the different levels of power-sharing involved. The third article in this volume is by Robert W. Hornaday, who presents experiences associated with introducing experiential learning techniques within a start-up MBA program in Myanmar. As such, it provides both insight into the transferability of this teaching technology to a foreign culture as well as suggesting its efficacy given the host country's cultural, economic, and religious background.

The article by Rebecca J. Morris provides a review of the use of another multicultural training in which students play the role of either international experts, citizens of the fictitious nation of Copernia, or anthropologists. In this exercise the international experts are hired by a foreign government to train its people, the Copernians, to manufacture hexaflexagons. This exercise has been useful in developing a sensitivity to cultural differences in task-oriented situations. The volume's last article by Scott D. Johnson, Denise M. Johnson and Peggy A. Golden deals with gender issues within an international-type business game. Given gender roles differ dramatically throughout the world, player expectations of each other should also vary, as well as should the benefits and rewards of simulation play. The authors document the degree to which gender influences perceptions, group structure and self-confidence, while fortunately for the game's application within gender-biased cultures, no significance on performance outcomes.

REFERENCES

Gosenpud, J. (1990). Evaluation of Experiential Learning. In J.W. Gentry (Ed.) *Guide to Business Gaming and Experiential Learning* (pp. 301-329) East Brunswick NJ: Nichols/GP Publishing.

Keys, B., and Wolfe, J. (1988). Management Education and Development: Current Issues and Emerging Trends, *1988 Yearly Review of Management* (Summer), 14 (2), 205-229.

Keys, B., and Wolfe, J. (1990). The Role of Management Games and Simulations in Education and Research, *1990 Yearly Review of Management* (Summer), 16 (2), 307-336.

Wexley, K.N., and Baldwin, T.T. (1986). Management Development, *1986 Yearly Review of Management* (Summer), 12 (2), 277-294.

Wolfe, J. (1990). The Evaluation of Computer-Based Business Games: Methodology, Findings, and Future Needs. In J.W. Gentry (Ed.) *Guide to Business Gaming and Experiential Learning* (pp. 279-300) East Brunswick NJ: Nichols/GP Publishing.

Prosperity Game (U.S.)
to Teach Global Competitiveness
to University Students

A23
F23 F02
C70

Kevin W. Boyack

Marshall Berman

SUMMARY. A Prosperity Game was designed and conducted to provide an experiential learning alternative to traditional lecture-based
course material in a first-year MBA class. The students played US and
Japanese business, government, and other roles, and experienced ethical, political, social, financial, and competitiveness issues in the context of a global marketplace. Student journals provided an indication
of the success of the method through comments that described the
depth of experiential learning in a simulation environment. *[Article
copies available for a fee from The Haworth Document Delivery Service:
1-800-342-9678. E-mail address: getinfo@ haworth.com]*

BACKGROUND

A Prosperity Game is a new type of forum for exploring complex issues
in a variety of areas including economics, politics, sociology, environment,
education, research, etc. The issues can be examined from a variety of

Kevin W. Boyack is a Senior Member of Technical Staff in the Innovative
Alliances Department at Sandia National Laboratories. Marshall Berman is Manager of the Innovative Alliances Department at Sandia National Laboratories.

This work was supported by the U.S. Department of Energy under Contract
DE-AC04-76DP00789.

[Haworth co-indexing entry note]: "Prosperity Game to Teach Global Competitiveness to University Students." Boyack, Kevin W., and Marshall Berman. Co-published simultaneously in *Journal of
Teaching in International Business* (International Business Press, an imprint of The Haworth Press, Inc.)
Vol. 8, No. 4, 1997, pp. 5-19; and: *Business Simulations, Games and Experiential Learning in International Business Education* (ed: Joseph Wolfe, and J. Bernard Keys) International Business Press, an
imprint of The Haworth Press, Inc., 1997, pp. 5-19. Single or multiple copies of this article are available
for a fee from The Haworth Document Delivery Service [1-800-342-9678, 9:00 a.m. - 5:00 p.m. (EST).
E-mail address: getinfo@haworth.com].

perspectives ranging from a global, macroeconomic and geopolitical view-point down to the details of customer/supplier/market interactions in specific industries.

Prosperity Games are an outgrowth of move/countermove and seminar war games, and originated from discussions among senior government people, industry representatives and management from Sandia National Laboratories. These games are executive-level interactive simulations that explore complex issues in a variety of economic, political, and social arenas. Prosperity Games are not computer games, but are high-level exercises of discretion, judgment, planning and negotiating skills.

To date, we have designed and conducted fourteen Prosperity Games on various topics including global competitiveness, electronics manufacturing, environmental technology and regulation, biomedical technology, university business school education, diversity and cultural change, and the restructuring of the Department of Energy and its National Laboratories. The general objectives of all these games have been to: stimulate thinking; develop relationships and partnerships among industry, government, labs, universities, and public groups; explore long-term strategies and policies; lay the foundation for industrial roadmaps; and provide informed input for possible future legislation.

The University Prosperity Game was the ninth of the fourteen games that we have conducted. It was held in conjunction with the Anderson Schools of Management at the University of New Mexico during April 1995. The scenario for this Prosperity Game was initially designed for the roadmap-making effort of the National Electronics Manufacturing Initiative (NEMI) of the Electronics Subcommittee of the Civilian Industrial Technology Committee under the aegis of the National Science and Technology Council (Berman, Berry, and VanDevender 1995). The game was modified to support course material in a first-year level MBA class dealing with the "Ethical, Political, and Social Environment of Business." In this context its main objectives were to: introduce and teach global competitiveness and business cultures in an experiential classroom setting; explore ethical, political, and social issues and address them in the context of global markets and competition; and obtain non-government views regarding the technical and policy issues developed in the NEMI roadmap-making endeavor.

UNIVERSITY PROSPERITY GAME DESCRIPTION

Game Scenario–SAMSON

The game scenario focuses on an imaginary electronics product called SAMSON, a high-tech personal communicator/entertainment/computer device. Although a current version of SAMSON exists, the final lightweight, portable advanced product will require hundreds of millions of dollars to commercialize. The current product is being developed and manufactured or imported by two companies, one American and one Japanese. The SAMSON product also has military applications and is viewed by the US Administration as being strategically important. The product is in the middle stage of development, but several key technologies need major innovation for the advanced technology to be successfully commercialized.

SAMSON is a spin-off of a military global battlefield communication device. The military product is currently very expensive and has limited capability. The ultimate consumer product is envisioned to have full-color 3-D displays, bio-sensor interfaces, voice and pattern recognition, global communications, global positioning/location, video and audio links, remote banking, etc. The current product is limited by weight and power consumption, has a black-and-white 3-D display, and no bio-interfaces. Additionally, a large investment in artificial intelligence software will be required. The key technical challenges are in software, human interfaces (tactile feedback, sensory inputs), color displays, low-power peripherals, and mass storage devices.

The US Administration is about to submit its budget request for the next fiscal year and is willing to consider financial support to SAMSON-type projects, but is uncertain what the best financial levers are; it has requested corporate input and a five-year technology development/commercialization plan. The US Administration must work within severe budget constraints as well as new treaties such as the General Agreement on Tariffs and Trade (GATT) and the North American Free Trade Agreement (NAFTA). The Japanese government requires similar information and has similar constraints.

Description of Roles

This game was designed for approximately 33-35 players, with 5 teams and 19 individual roles, as shown in Table 1. The teams represent the executive management committees of each of 5 companies and are composed of 3 players each. The individual roles primarily reflect the government and public sectors including various legislative and agency (or Ministry) officials, laboratories, universities, finance, the media, and the customer/taxpayer, both in the US and Japan. The Control Team oversees game play and represents the rest of the world.

The five company teams are Infomatics, a US electronics and computer manufacturer; Horioka, a Japanese robotics, electronics and computer man-

TABLE 1. Roles: Teams and Individuals

US Roles	Japanese Roles
Infomatics (team)	Horioka (team)
Mechatronics (team)	Viewall (team)
US Senator	Int'l Trade Policy Bureau (MITI[+]) Official
US Representative	Industrial Policy Bureau (MITI[+]) Official
Dept. of Energy/Defense Official	Machinery & Info. Ind. Bureau (MITI[+]) Official
Dept. of Commerce Official	Minister of Finance
US Laboratory/University Official	Minister of Posts and Telecommunications
US Financier	Minister of Foreign Affairs
US Distributor	Japanese Banker
US Activist	Japanese Distributor
US Media	Japanese Media
US Worker/Consumer	

Other Roles
Rootska (team)
Control Team

[+] MITI - Ministry of International Trade and Industry

ufacturer; Mechatronics, a small US firm specializing in robotics; Viewall, a Japanese display manufacturer; and Rootska, a Ukrainian software company.

The business world comprises interactions between companies, government agencies and officials, and other members of the public and private sectors. Each role faces many ethical, political, and social issues in the course of its dealings, in addition to the financial and competitiveness issues traditionally associated with the business world. This game was designed to explore many of these interactions with students playing the roles. Initial challenges and conflicts were built into the detailed descriptions of each team and individual role. Challenges for the Japanese roles were assembled with the aid of staff at the University of New Mexico

US-Japan Center and Mr. Manabu Eto, a visiting scholar and Ministry of International Trade and Industry (MITI) official. The detailed role descriptions and initial challenges are available elsewhere (Boyack and Berman 1996).

For company roles, students were to assume that intra-company issues had been delegated to subordinates, so their work would guide the company as a whole. The actions of each team were subject to the discipline of a working consensus; i.e., every member of the team could live with the corporate consensus position and no member of the team could do anything that is unacceptable to any other member of the team. Therefore, it was not necessary (but was allowed) to establish manager-subordinate roles within teams.

Game Outline and Rules

The University Prosperity Game was conducted over a four-week period of time during which the class met once per week for two-and-one-half hours. The final hour of the first class period was spent explaining the game, distributing handbooks, and answering preliminary questions. The students were to read the handbooks for general information over the next few days. Roles were assigned two days before the next class period, rather than when handbooks were distributed, so that the students would have greater reason to read the entire handbook. This allowed two days for each student to develop a detailed understanding of their assigned role, issues, and potential interactions.

Preparatory to the start of the second period each team or individual was asked to take some time to define objectives for the future, i.e., ask the question "Where should this individual or company be in five or ten years?" The first hour of the second class period was set aside for strategizing and planning. Each role was to spend this time in defining overall strategies, potential moves and negotiations to enact those strategies, and planned responses to the initial challenges inherent in their roles. The remainder of the second period was available for interaction and negotiation between any parties on any issue. Time was prescribed to update at the rate of two years per half class period. The classroom was divided into US and Japanese regions that were separated by a row of tables representing the ocean.

Interactions and negotiations between parties outside of class during the week were encouraged. The third class period was conducted as an extension of the second period, in which further strategizing, interaction, and negotiation were allowed. Game play was terminated at the end of the third class period.

Current (both true and false) information was injected into the game through the roles of the news media. These individuals were allowed to roam freely and assemble any information they desired using any method. Each was then allowed to "broadcast" their news orally to the group each hour.

Money and influence were included in the game. Each role was assigned initial assets in the form of dollars and influence credits to use during the second class period. The Control Team reviewed the game play between the second and third class periods, and assigned each role additional assets for the third class period. Players had two ways in which they could alter the future. Dollars and credits could be used to achieve progress, either through negotiation (e.g., contracting R&D on a certain component) or through the exercise of a Toolkit that was designed for this game. The Toolkit is explained in the following section.

A few formal rules were issued to the students. One rule was that any agreement between parties whether involving an exchange of assets or not, in order to be valid in the game, must be in writing on a special agreement form provided for that purpose, and must be signed by a member of the Control Team. This was necessary to allow the Control Team to track the flow of the game. For grading purposes, students were required to keep journals of their game play, in which they were instructed to record their interactions, reasons for decisions, feelings, and any insights gained.

The fourth class period was used as a debriefing session, in which students were given three to five minutes to recap their experience. This gave the students an opportunity to know what was happening in different parts of the game and gave them an overall perspective on the outcome. In addition, these debriefings helped them to better understand the full context under which they made decisions, and why certain outcomes occurred.

Technology and Policy Toolkit

The Toolkit is an integral part of the Prosperity Games concept, and is a vehicle which allows for progress in this complex technical and information-driven world to be simulated in the game without foreknowledge of certain events. Another purpose of the Toolkit is to examine the effects of potential options in the context of simulated but real-world industrial and government policies and actions. For this game, the Toolkit was a subset of that used in the NEMI game (Berman, Berry, and VanDevender 1995). Each potential technology and policy change was termed an option. Technology options provided opportunities for investment to enable potential upgrades or breakthroughs in technology, while policy options were suggested changes that were thought to enable increased competitiveness. The game designers assigned a total resource investment (dollars and/or credits) to each option that would yield a 50% probability of success.

Success, defined as reaching the desired outcome, was not assured beforehand, regardless of the resources allocated; a desired outcome could not be bought outright. However, we assumed that the probability of success would increase with an increase in the resources allocated. For the Toolkit, success or failure (achieving or not achieving the desired outcome) of each option was determined probabilistically as shown in Figure 1. First, the baseline probability was calculated using a normal cumulative probability distribution with mean x and standard deviation $\sigma = x$. Hence, an investment of twice the mean would yield a success probability of 0.84. To take into account factors other than total investment, a uniform distribution was superimposed on the normal distribution to reflect uncertainties and risks in the real world for accomplishing major technology or policy breakthroughs. This uniform distribution could increase the baseline probability by as much as 16% or decrease it by as much as 32%, as shown by the dashed lines in Figure 1. Success or failure was then determined by generation of a random number between zero and one. If the random number was less than the investment probability, the option

FIGURE 1. Probability of Successful Toolkit Option for Cumulative Investments

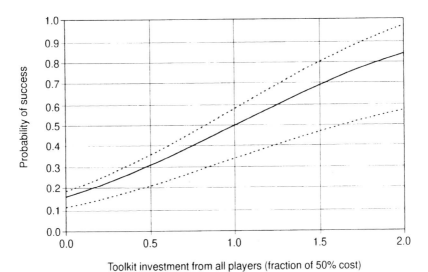

Toolkit investment from all players (fraction of 50% cost)

succeeded; otherwise it failed. When a Toolkit option succeeded, its immediate effect was estimated by the Control Team and was relayed to all roles affected by the change.

RESULTS AND OBSERVATIONS

Prosperity Games are games of discretion and judgment and, therefore, need to be analyzed in the context of human interaction. In previous games, analysts observed each team's actions and recorded their understanding of the underlying dynamics. With the many individual roles in this game, using analysts was impractical. As mentioned previously, to provide similar information for analysis of this game, the students were each required to keep a journal in which they were asked to record their thoughts, feelings, observations, reasoning for decisions, and what they learned. These journals, together with observations from the game staff and a record of formal agreements, have provided a wealth of information regarding the dynamics of the game.

Success in meeting the game's objectives can be directly inferred from comments in many of the students' journals. Quotes from the journals are given here as evidence. The full set of student journals are available in Boyack and Berman (1996).

Teaching Global Competitiveness

The game was very effective at teaching global competitiveness and business cultures. The University Prosperity Game was used as an alternative to the traditional lecture-based method of teaching concepts related to global competitiveness. These concepts are internalized due to the experiential nature of their presentation. One student stated it this way:

> The Prosperity Game is a great way to stimulate thinking and teach global competitiveness . . . Overall, [it] was a great learning tool. I enjoyed the interaction with other roles, especially the negotiating and implementing strategies.

Another student elaborated even more.

> By doing this role playing game, I feel we get a little experience about what it is like to operate in the global market. The confusion we first felt must be similar to what the real individuals feel when

confronted with similar problems. What actions can I take to better my position? What should be my position? How much should I spend? These types of questions are hard to deal with.

Another commented that this was "macro business on a micro scale. This was a good lesson in the dynamics of international business. [I have a] much better appreciation and understanding of Japanese business practices."

In addition to learning about global dynamics and culture, some students learned about the depth of business dealings and tools that can be used to accomplish business goals.

> The game is over, and I've learned tons. So much goes on in a business deal such as Viewall's 3-D technology and I now realize to what extent one must go to get desired results.

> It was amazing how deep some of the deals could go to satisfy so many parties.

> [I] learned ability/importance of using influence and external sources to achieve major success!

One student also commented that "odd partnerships form and playing field and rules change rapidly." This is certainly the case in the international arena, and the students had the experience of dealing with this complexity rather than just reading about it.

Exposure to Ethical, Political and Social Issues

The game involved students in ethical, political and social issues in an experiential business setting. Several teams were confronted with ethical issues, particularly involving espionage. In one case, a team was approached to participate in an espionage option. Their response: "We (Infomatics) agree that it is not something in which we would like to be involved. It goes against our company's ethical principles."

By contrast, Viewall exercised a Toolkit option to acquire (through espionage) a critical display technology from a European company. One of the team members had the following view.

> I believe purchasing stolen technology to be ethically wrong. Period. But at the time, it seemed like the only course of action open to us. We had our back against the wall because no one wanted to help finance our research into newer technologies . . . I feel the decision to get the stolen technology to have been the correct move to make.

Clearly, this student adopted the ethics that he associated with the role, rather than imposing his own ethics on the situation. This facet of game play naturally creates conflict within a person. Each must decide how to play a role, either by assuming one's perception of the role, or superimposing one's personality on it. "It forced me to look at how I behave when I have a specific role to play and how I can and will manipulate that role to fit my personality."

The Viewall situation also pointed out that what is ethical may vary from culture to culture. This point was made by one of the media players.

> Though unethical by American standards, I don't think they felt they were doing anything wrong. In fact, to the contrary, they were simply using every means at their disposal to move ahead in the market.

Ethics were also an issue in the political side of the game. One US politician experienced the conflict that might occur between ethics and desired outcomes.

> My actions as a politician may have been a little slimy, but I truly believe they were in the best interest of the country. I just realized that most real politicians probably think the same thing.

Traditional social issues in areas such as labor and the environment did not take a front seat in this game. Although an environmental issue was included in the game design, and was acted upon by several parties, the predominant social issues addressed by the students were those dealing with relationships and communication. In the words of one student: "This game is about TRUST. How do people make decisions . . . form contracts . . . cooperate . . . aggregate power . . . in the middle of so much activity, tension and unknown factors?"

Others learned that communications are key.

> Even more difficult is dealing with other people. It was hard to convince people to do certain things even if, in the long run, they would benefit from those actions.

> The lessons learned from this exercise basically are that relations not only between two countries are complicated, but also between individuals who desire the same goal but who go about achieving it differently. In order to accomplish anything, constant dialog is necessary.

The game was structured with few rules about what the students could and could not do. For some, this lack of structure was a challenge, yet one made use of the opportunity to learn valuable lessons about success.

> I feel good about the game now. I can see that there really are no rules, and we do what we must, with certain notations, to reach our goals. The problem is conflicting goals, and conflicting groups, with conflicting purposes, and (sometimes) conflicting personalities.

Others experienced a great change in their perception of the world and level of interest in the issues around them as a result of this experience.

> While watching the national news last night, I realized how much more aware and analytical I have become about so many issues. This class has truly been mind expanding; I'm much more interested in certain issues than I used to be, such as politics, economics, environment (maybe because I'm starting to understand some of it?) and I realize how truly interrelated everything is. Because of our game I'm also more aware that you can't always believe what the media says . . . [The] game taught me to think more critically.

Difficulty of Playing Foreign Roles

As the game progressed, it became clear that there was a difference in the level of activity on the US and Japanese sides of the classroom. Those playing Japanese roles were noticeably more frustrated with the game. We attribute this to the difficulty of playing a foreign role. The American culture and lifestyle is very ingrained in most college-aged people of US origin. This makes basing decisions on a foreign culture and set of values very difficult, and leads to internal conflict in many cases. As stated by one student:

> You can read all you want about a culture, but you have to live it to truly understand and learn it. I don't mean a two week visit, I mean a few months. So I don't think reading some material truly gave me insight to the Japanese culture; therefore, I could not help but act with American mentality.

One Oriental student was more precise about how a detailed knowledge and internalization of the culture is required to play a role convincingly.

> The people who played Japanese roles did not act like Japanese. They should be more unified. The government should show more

power in direct business operations. Japan is a country in which a government has the capability to create a consensus in society that is sufficient to allow government to design and implement goals for the community as a whole, change the behavior of important groups such as business, change the structure of society.

At the end of the debriefing session, the students were given surveys to determine their feelings about various aspects of the game. Some of the questions were specific to this University game, while others were general questions we have used for all Prosperity Games. Responses were based on a scale of "1 = very little" to "3 = neutral" to "5 = very much." Although the survey was anonymous, we asked the students to state the nationality of the role they played. This allowed us to discover any differences due to role nationality. Mean responses to eleven of the questions are given in Table 2 for the US and Japanese role players (the Japanese group included one Ukrainian response) along with the statistical level of significance corresponding to the differences in the means. The level of significance was calculated based on the test of equality of two means, with the assumption that variances were known. Only those questions where the difference in the means was significant to greater than 90% are shown in the table.

The absolute values of the responses were generally high, indicating overall satisfaction with the game. However, the significant differences between US and Japanese mean responses is a strong indicator that the difficulty of playing foreign roles negatively affected the perceived effectiveness of the game to those who played them.

Particularly interesting are the responses to questions 4, 7 and 11. Each of these questions reflects primarily on the interactions within regions, since there was little inter-regional negotiation during the game. In real life, the keiretsu structure presumes that company-to-company interdependence and trust among peers in the Japanese culture would be high. However, in the game, the students found it difficult to create that structure given their predominantly American heritage, despite the presence of Mr. Eto, who was available to answer questions and help organize the Japanese effort. By contrast, without the pressure of playing a role by foreign rules, the American role players worked together more and developed a higher level of trust.

Questions 5 and 9 reflect on the quality of information and comfort level for each nationality. The US roles were slightly more refined due to the greater availability of information and the familiarity of the game designers with American culture.

TABLE 2. Mean Responses to Polling Questions from US and Japanese Role Players

	US	Japanese	Δ_{means}
1. Did the game broaden your perspective?	4.53	3.87	0.66[***]
2. How well did the game meet your objectives?	4.21	3.40	0.81[**]
3. Did the game stimulate future thinking?	4.20	3.47	0.73[**]
4. Did the game simulate real life?	4.27	3.60	0.67[**]
5. Rate the Player's Handbook.	3.33	2.73	0.60[*]
6. How well did the game meet the sponsors' objectives?	4.14	3.47	0.67[*]
7. How much do you trust your peers (classmates)?	4.07	3.53	0.54[*]
8. Did the game maintain your interest and enthusiasm?	4.57	4.00	0.57[*]
9. Rate the game format.	3.53	3.00	0.53[*]
10. Did the game explore long-term planning?	3.80	3.27	0.53[†]
11. How willing are people to consider company to company interdependence despite potentially adversarial relationships?	3.47	2.93	0.54[†]

Level of significance [†] $p < 0.10$, [*] $p < 0.05$, [**] $p < 0.01$, [***] $p < 0.001$

Other Game Highlights

The students exhibited substantial innovation and creativity toward the end of game play. Some of this resulted from attempts to break the rules due to the frustration that developed in a fast-paced environment. In the technology area, the students proposed their own Toolkit options to develop advanced virtual-reality interfaces and brainwave interfaces to the SAMSON device. In the organizational area, a US technology delivery system was proposed and won wide acceptance among the US role players. This organization was set up with funding from the private companies, as well as the legislature and other government agencies. This joint funding was then used to invest in research and development of technologies of interest to the majority of the group, and that would position the US more strongly in the global marketplace. The one inter-regional development was a merger between the US and Japanese distributors of SAMSON devices to form a global distribution company. This gave them the power to deal with both SAMSON manufacturers as they chose with little fear of retribution.

We found in this game, as well as in others that we have conducted (Berman, Boyack, and VanDevender 1995), that proposed role switches are met with great resistance. This is especially true on teams, where bonding occurs very quickly among players who had little or no interaction before the game. It is easier to facilitate a role switch between individuals (we used an election on the US side after a scandal in the legislature was revealed), especially if one sees this switch as a way to increase status or power in the game.

Lessons Learned

Both we and the students learned many things from this game. As game designers, we learned that the Players' Handbook and verbal instructions must be simpler and more explanatory. There needs to be a significant time at the beginning of the game to provide that explanation and verbally lead the students through short examples of facets of traditional game play. The game needs to be revised to provide greater rewards for look-ahead strategies and greater penalties for mistakes. This will promote learning through the emotions induced by knowledge of potential consequences.

The students learned about the importance of preparation and strategic planning. Those roles in which the students invested a significant effort in preparation either prior to or during the second class period controlled the flow of the game. Those who did not invest this effort played the game in a reactive fashion. Many students also learned about the importance of agreements. Verbal agreements are not traceable, and often different parties have different views of what comprised a verbal agreement. Agreements must be very specific as to what each party gives and receives. The language of the agreement is important and must be very clear. Time pressures are no excuse for writing agreements with inadequate detail.

CONCLUSION

The comments in the students' journals, of which only a few are presented here, are strong evidence that the teaching objectives of the game were met. In the words of one student: "[This was] really an interesting experience; best project I've done in the MBA program (I'm almost done)."

The conflict and emotion created by a well-designed simulation environment, combined with the urgency of time pressures, give rise to an experience that is internalized by the students to a very high degree. This thought is echoed by the professor in whose class we conducted the game.

Experiential learning is more effective than the typical classroom methods of communicating information. The [Prosperity] Game was a creative way to stimulate multi-dimensional learning . . . All in all, an excellent simulation that achieved learning objectives better than any alternatives I have used.

Due to its nature, the University Prosperity Game can be easily modified to support course material in many different business courses, by limiting or adding roles, and by changing the initial challenges for each role. We plan to modify the current game version in response to the lessons learned and use it in other educational and business settings.

REFERENCES

Berman, M., Berry, I. and VanDevender, J. P. (1995). *Prosperity Game for the National Electronics Manufacturing Initiative*. Sandia National Laboratories Report SAND95-0724, Albuquerque, New Mexico.

Berman, M., Boyack, K. W. and VanDevender, J. P. (1995). *Environmental Prosperity Game*. Sandia National Laboratories Report SAND95-2701, Albuquerque, New Mexico.

Boyack, K. W. and Berman, M. (1996). *University Prosperity Game*. Sandia National Laboratories Report SAND96-0562, Albuquerque, New Mexico.

From Benevolent Dictator to Constitutional Monarch: Simulating a European Works Council in a U.S. Classroom

Jeremiah J. O'Connell

SUMMARY. Frustration with didactic methods in teaching American students about European-style "participation" led to the use of a semester-long simulation of a European works council in a graduate cross-cultural course. Students shaped in the American culture of person-centered, direct participation learned by living an institutionalized, representational participation system. A written class council charter contractually bound both instructor and students to power-sharing via redefined roles in the management of the class. Student testimony documents the effectiveness of this simulation in driving learning to previously unreached levels. *[Article copies available for a fee from The Haworth Document Delivery Service: 1-800-342-9678. E-mail address: getinfo@haworth.com]*

INTRODUCTION

Anyone who has tried to teach cross-culturally about employee "participation" has undoubtedly found the word to be heavily value-laden. Having split my teaching career between the U.S. and Europe, I have encoun-

Jeremiah J. O'Connell is Professor of Management at Bentley College.

[Haworth co-indexing entry note]: "From Benevolent Dictator to Constitutional Monarch: Simulating a European Works Council in a U.S. Classroom." O'Connell, Jeremiah J. Co-published simultaneously in *Journal of Teaching in International Business* (International Business Press, an imprint of The Haworth Press, Inc.) Vol. 8, No. 4, 1997, pp. 21-38; and: *Business Simulations, Games and Experiential Learning in International Business Education* (ed: Joseph Wolfe, and J. Bernard Keys) International Business Press, an imprint of The Haworth Press, Inc., 1997, pp. 21-38. Single or multiple copies of this article are available for a fee from The Haworth Document Delivery Service [1-800-342-9678, 9:00 a.m. - 5:00 p.m. (EST). E-mail address: getinfo@haworth.com].

tered no slipperier concept. The differing values and beliefs underlying the concept often don't show on the surface. Heads nod knowingly on each side of the Atlantic, but appreciation for the shared meaning comes with great difficulty. Lecturing about the differences in meaning may achieve some knowledge transfer but leaves unchanged the students' capacity to explain, much less to critique or evaluate "participation" as understood and practiced on each side of the Atlantic. Certainly, lecturing does little if anything to help the students to become more effective in behaving "participatively" outside their own cultural context. After years of under-achievement with these deeper and more challenging learning objectives, I successfully invested in a semester-long experiential method with gradu-ate students in the U.S. taking a cross-cultural comparative management course. Our learning community simulated "participation," European-style, as the chief vehicle for reaching meaningful knowledge, attitude, as well as skill objectives.

The pages which follow specify two content issues. First, I explain the differing meanings of "participation" with their cultural roots. Second, I argue for the appropriateness of utilizing so extensive a simulation in this context. The balance of this article then documents the simulation process along with initial and final student commentaries. I conclude with a dis-cussion, drawn from successive running of the simulation, of the educa-tional risks and rewards of investing in the kind of simulation which transforms the classroom from the domain of a benevolent dictator to that of a constitutional monarch. Prince John at Runneymede somewhat reluc-tantly played revolutionary 780 years ago when he acceded to the de-mands of the barons with the Magna Charta. The simulation described here would have the instructor voluntarily reshape her/his own comfort-able classroom domain to a more risky, less predictable, community for the sake of worthy learning objectives. Princess Jean or Prince John, are you out there?

THE CONTENT ISSUES

"Participation," U.S.-style, appears in our texts (see, for instance, Bowditch and Buono, 1994:402) as a matter of personal style in the bilat-eral relationship between superior and subordinate. In the U.S. phenome-non seen with European optics, the style is person-centered, guaranteed by trust, and motivated by the utilitarian conviction that, modally, Y works better than X. When one questions the basis for the pragmatic belief, Argyris, Maslow or McGregor would argue the case of the human needs of the subordinate—a psychological rationale. Even in the later calculus of contingency theory, "participation" remained the top-down choice made after examining task, situational, and personal variables in a real-time, what-works-best-now optimization. The calculus could change tomorrow or with a different subordinate. The more modern empowerment version, when all the language gets stripped away, leaves the superior as dictator who gives and takes away as she/he decides (Ford and Fottler, 1995). Substituting for the "boss/subordinate" language, the politically correct "associate" label does not change the hierarchic reality in the U.S. employment-at-will environment. This is clear in Tannenbaum's (1986) analysis of the debate about control or power and participation.

European "participation" (1) has an entirely different feel, especially for the U.S. observer. European "participation" has the character of institutional, multi-lateral, representational, system-centered, guaranteed in law, and based on moral rights—much more a political science construct than one from psychology (Levinson, 1974:56). Whatever style the co-worker (boss/subordinate equivalent language does not exist in German, Dutch or Swedish) utilizes, the nonmanagerial colleague is assured of some level of participation in virtually all decisions. Calori and Dufour (1995:63) describe this phenomenon as "a higher level of internal negotiation." Figure 1 displays the differing levels of legislated employee involvement in Germany, for instance (from a very weak form at the bottom of the vertical axis to very strong at the top), on a continuum of management decisions (from relatively important decisions at the left of the horizontal axis to relatively unimportant decisions on the right), compared to typical practice in the U.S. even in unionized companies.

Works councils in Germany serve as the vehicles for only part of the participation pictured in Figure 1. The system of participation institutions includes the board of directors as well as the collective bargaining mechanisms (Kolvenbach and Hanau, 1987:5-46).

American students, especially those with some early career work experience, carry with them the person-centered concept of U.S. "participation." Surprisingly, with 80% or more of the American students having come through unionized primary schools, secondary schools, and even universities, the institutionalized version of employee participation has not shaped their values and beliefs on the subject. Their expectations at work reflect as much attraction for Y and inclination for X as their parents. It appears, too, that west winds from across the Atlantic have not yet contaminated mainstream values and beliefs with sufficient innovations like union membership on the Chrysler board of directors (an inspiration from the German I. G. Metal union) and self-managed production teams (à la Volvo from Sweden). Evidently, practices can be borrowed cross-culturally with-

FIGURE 1. Power Sharing Levels and Decision Hierarchy

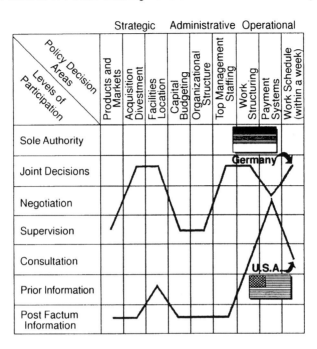

out the attendant values and beliefs baggage. American students, on learning about European participation from reading or lectures, most often find it curious and are skeptical that the system can be made to work. They have difficulty appreciating the European values and beliefs about human rights, organizational forms, and the legitimate role of government in shaping management practice in private enterprise (for more contrasting values and beliefs, see O'Connell, 1984). My students always seemed to come away from their study with a flawed appreciation for this strange phenomenon. "That's interesting" as a learning outcome hardly approaches the threshold of education in international management at my school. I had to do better.

In content terms, the relevance of experiential methods, especially this extensive simulation, in this kind of course deserves some further discussion. Experiential methods already appeared in this course. The BAFA BAFA exercise served well as an ice breaker and vehicle for beginning the consideration of the challenge of becoming cross-culturally effective managers. Throughout the course as well, students engaged in role plays within case discussions. Still, in these experiential events, we jumped into and out of roles within very short times and scarcely had to live at all with the consequences of our behavior in role. To do better with the "participation" issue, a longer and more rigorous role play or "participatory modelling" (Walck, 1992:34) would be necessary to allow practice time in role and feedback about personal effectiveness. The students had to experience consequences beyond a larger handful of blue or green chips or a greater number of single color cards in sequence. Gunz (1995:58) insists that students experiment in a risk-free environment. On the contrary, wouldn't the presence of risk heighten what Kolb (1985) called "reflective observation" of the "concrete experience?" They—we—had to risk more to gain more. We had to live with the consequences—important consequences to both instructor and students—of our new role behaviors. That would take time. That would take role definitions that *permanently* reshuffled the organizational deck. Little (1990) discusses the benefits of semester-long "character immersion" role plays which are analogous to our simulation, except that our roles did not end. At issue in these role play encounters would have to be something as mutually important as the grade. Prince John would have to volunteer to go to Runneymede and deliver a new Magna Charta to his student barons.

The Magna Charta in this case was the Class Council Charter (Exhibit A). Just as the syllabus serves as a contract between instructor and students, the Class Council Charter has the character of contract. The Charter adopts the language, structure, and procedures of half-century-old European participation systems (see Exhibit B for the inspiration of the different features of the Charter). This contract between the instructor and students fundamentally and permanently altered the relationship in dramatic ways. The presence of an elected council interposed a representative body into what had been a face-to-face, bilateral relationship. It threw open the classroom doors by redefining the system boundaries, introducing third parties (Dean's office, arbitration panel of students not enrolled in this particular section, and a lawyer/arbitrator) into important roles. The formally all-powerful instructor would now have to defer (under closely defined terms) to the Class Council, to the arbitration panel, and to the lawyer/arbitrator. The instructor's former unilateral authority would henceforth be constrained by precisely defined solo decision competence, consultation, and information rights held by the Class Council. Students too would find their former ease in attempting to finesse the instructor one-on-one would be complicated by Class Council involvement as advisor on such things as late paper submission, and the like. Pluralism raised the uncertainty factor and extended the time required for the decision process. In the newly designed environment there was much more the feel of rule of law than rule of man. The prince and barons found themselves in a constitutionally-determined structure as unfamiliar and threatening as it was intriguing and promising.

THE SIMULATION PROCESS

The context for the simulation was an elective MBA course (Cross-Cultural Comparative Management) with one prerequisite, the basic management/OB (Organizational Behavior) course. Every semester we were blessed with rich diversity in the class enrollment (2).

The simulation process began at the beginning of the first class meeting when the students received a copy of the course syllabus and a copy of the Class Council Charter. In seconds, the students uncovered that the syllabus contained no "requirements and grading" section. Instead, the syllabus stated: "Evaluation Process: the mix of bases for evaluation, the format for each, the scheduling for each, and the relative weight of each in the final grade will be co-determined by the Class Council and the instructor." In minutes, without any reference by the instructor to simulation or experiential learning methods, the realization struck that this class would be different from the norm in strange ways. Even a quick reading of the Class Council Charter revealed unfamiliar language and unusual procedures, the first of which was an election for Class Council members to be conducted before the end of the first class session. Seldom have students listened so attentively to the self introductions of men and women from whom they would have to nominate and elect Class Council members charged with playing significant roles in structuring so central an issue as the grading system for this class. In reviewing the syllabus, I made no connection between the institution of an elected and mandated Class Council and the three classes dedicated to European employee participation in weeks 11, 12, and 13. This was to be discovery learning until the debriefing of the simulation during that section of the syllabus some 70 days hence.

Perceiving their having no choice, the students followed the Class Council Charter in nominating six classmates from the six constituencies based on gender, nationality, and student status as full- or part-time. The women and men separated and each chose a nominee. Then the international students and U.S. students did likewise, as then did the full- and part-time students. After the nominees stood to be identified, the class voted by secret ballot. The tellers performed the count and announced the four top vote getters, obviating the need for the tie-breaking routine. I encouraged the class to discuss the evaluation process with their elected representatives before the instructor and Class Council met outside of class to co-determine the system in time for presentation at the third class. The second class period was to be totally dedicated to the BAFA BAFA exercise.

When the Council met in my office eight days later, they elected a chairperson on the first ballot. After much discussion with managers who had extensive experience interacting with European works councils, I knew much time could be saved if I offered to provide a menu of evaluation system ideas for consideration, much as a staff resource person might to a committee. The Council debated among themselves and tested my tolerance for variances in the system elements, for instance, reducing the weight for class participation close to zero. I freely expressed opinion and even held out for some form of peer evaluation as part of the class participation grading process. All the while, Council complained that they were unsure of their constituencies' wishes, pushing for more time to test ideas with the class and even to hold populist-style straw ballots. I pushed for closure in time for the presentation of the final system in proper written form to the class during the third class to be held within the next week. After some hemming and hawing, Council voted, without the need for the chairperson's tie breaker, on each element of the evaluation system (see Exhibit C, part I). As the Council moved on to other decisions (see Exhibit C, part II) on which they had independent competence (I was present only to remind them of the decisions to be made), they fell into the executive mode without further talk of their absent constituencies.

In the third class meeting, the Council Chairperson distributed the evaluation system and described its contents. The only question was "Can we propose changes?" To which the chairperson authoritatively responded: "No." Overall reaction must have been satisfactory since no one proposed invoking the recall procedures from the Council Charter. Council's decisions concerning breaks, buzz groups, and class directory immediately shaped how we operated for the balance of the semester. Other than mid-course adjustments in the buzz groups, Council appeared only to record on the board the distribution of grades for the mid-term. Less visibly, the instructor consulted Council members on one student's request for a deadline delay for family reasons. The petitioner seemed taken back when I reminded him of my obligation to consult the Council before granting the request which otherwise would probably have been virtually automatic. Once I had to remind both a petitioner and the Council itself that Council was advisory only on student petitions. The student had come to me with the news that Council had granted an extension of a deadline. On one other occasion I consulted the Council members on the switching of two classes because of a change in schedule for one of our guest speakers. This time I informed the class that I was switching the two classes after consulting Council. Council called no special class meetings, and Council itself held whatever meetings it required without using class time. No one invoked the arbitration panel nor involved the lawyer/arbitrator.

In class eleven, after the students had read two articles on industrial democracy and workers' participation in management, I had the students express their personal attitudes toward the three dimensions of industrial democracy (power sharing, affluence sharing, and work humanizing) via a questionnaire. I compared their responses to samples of European executives and then engaged in a lecture/discussion of the values and beliefs in Europe which provided fertile ground for the emergence of industrial democracy institutions via legislation beginning soon after the second world war. It wasn't until the twelfth class meeting when I gave them readings (Kolvenbach and Hanau, 1987) and a lecture about the instruments of power sharing that our own experience with the simulated works council came up for discussion. A very rich discussion ensued and continued right into the thirteenth class when we discussed the lessons for U.S. managers from European-style participation. Students showed real sophistication in critiquing three articles (Ewing, 1981; Mills, 1976; and Saskin, 1984) whose authors saw great relevance to the U.S. from the European experience. Non-U.S. students played important roles in helping the class critically evaluate the prospects for the importation of European institutional forms across the Atlantic in face of the differences in values and beliefs. The greatest insight came in the discussion of the accommodations required of U.S. managers operating in Europe and European managers operating in the U.S. Council members inserted frequent references to their own experience as elected class representatives, especially in the debate about conscience versus constituency in decision making by the representatives.

In the debriefing of the works council simulation, class members expressed some concern of being cut out of the loop in the relationship between the Council members and the instructor (see Poole, 1986, for a discussion of representational issues). On the recommendation of these students, the Class Council Charter for the later running of the simulation called for the inclusion of two scheduled assemblies of class and Council without the instructor present. In these assemblies, information could be shared and Council could be held accountable by its constituencies. Such how-are-things-going sessions could also provide a speak-up vehicle for students who might be too shy to speak directly to the instructor.

At the end of the semester, students wrote anonymous reflections on the works council simulation. When asked about their feelings that first evening when they read the Class Council Charter, the students focused a great deal on their preoccupation with the grading system. Both the promise and the anxiety showed in their responses.

- He's trying something new and different. . . . I support risk taking according to specific guidelines . . . a superb way to take cognitive leaps.
- I thought it was great . . . very democratic . . . certainly a refreshing perspective considering the fixed grading policies of other classes.
- I thought it was different, yet interesting. . . . I was excited to deviate from the norm and participate in this different structure. . . . I really didn't know what to expect.
- Some concern, slight fear, but very interested to see how it would work.
- I felt it was very strange and had no idea where it was heading.
- At first I was very skeptical. Although I viewed it as a wonderful opportunity to participate in a system I had often criticized, my fear of the unknown made me hesitate. Soon, I was very excited about seeing it through.
- At first, I was a little confused because I didn't know what the implications could be and how much involvement the Council would really have.
- I was shocked. At first, I didn't understand why the professor would be interested in allowing the students to have input on how the class was run. Then I thought it was really cool.
- Different, radical, but not outrageous for a graduate school course.
- Initially I did not like the idea . . . didn't fully understand the impact.
- Skepticism and reluctance.
- Quite surprised and reluctant. I was also skeptical as to whether the approach would work in such an environment.
- Confusion. I wondered immediately how I was going to be evaluated. To be honest, I did not like the idea at first. It brought too much uncertainty.
- You must be crazy! How can 35 people decide on so many subjects and get consensus?
- Really? No way! How does it work? How much power is actually shared?

Since concern for the grading system was of primary importance, I asked the students how they reacted after the announcement of the co-determined evaluation system. Students responded more positively but both skepticism and anxiety still remained.

- I liked it. I really liked the ability to adjust my requirements to fit my schedule and my tolerance for risk.
- I was shocked that each of us was able to pick which way we wanted to be graded. I had an uneasy feeling at first with this because I wasn't exactly sure the way I wanted to be graded. I feel more secure with having the rules already laid out. I was surprised I would like this form of participation.
- The fact I had the opportunity to choose what I wanted satisfied me greatly. I felt more in control of my evaluation process. I feel that I approach something that I brought on myself more positively than something I have been obliged to do.
- I was pleasantly surprised. I got more involved in the whole process. I was excited to see how I could control my grade. I was glad to see that we could rate class participation to the extent that we wanted because some people do speak more than others.
- It was very fair. I couldn't imagine, though, how an instructor could develop an evaluation that could honestly compare the amount of effort invested by one student over another.
- I was very excited about the outcome. I felt in control of my own destiny as far as the course was concerned.
- Still a little skeptical, "concerned," although at the same time interested.
- Still unsure as to what to expect. As we moved along, I began to feel that the flexibility was a bonus. It made me feel as though I had a voice in how the class I paid so much for was being conducted.

When questioned about the learning outcomes from the works council simulation, the students focused not only on what they experientially learned about European-style participation, but they also pointed to additional personal skill lessons and to motivational support for learning.

- It did bring home the issue of worker participation.
- I could relate to the material discussed in class. It was not some theory or concept out of reach.
- It may have mirrored real life with little contact or communication with the elected representatives or follow-up report or evaluation.
- Brought representation "home."

- It taught me a lot about civic duty. Having been given a position of power, one should use it for the good of the greatest number of people, not for personal gain.
- It helped me realize that in having rights you also have responsibility attached to those rights.
- It taught me or rather gave me some insights into managing choice and in managing representatives. You were a very positive role model as a manager of the process. Learning by doing is such a great teacher.
- Most importantly, that a system like this does work. More than one person can develop a system.
- It provided the opportunity to take responsibility for our own destiny in terms of what we wanted to learn, how we wanted to be measured, etc.
- It was great to see how my own decisions on grading affected my final grade.
- As a new learning process I was more interested in being part of the process, the class and the educational benefits.
- I discovered that I like this approach more than the standard approach. You become more involved as student and value the ability to control your own grading to some extent.
- Students seemed far more excited and *involved* in this course than they seemed in other courses.

When asked if this approach should be used again in this course, the students expressed a unanimously positive response. In doing so, they recommended modifications ranging from rotating Council membership to extension of Council prerogatives to codetermination of certain parts of the syllabus in terms of coverage.

RISKS AND REWARDS

The classroom is a nonsymmetrical world. The instructor clearly bears most of the risk of the simulation and exerts most of the energy in adapting to the innovations produced in the co-determined evaluation system. It's her/his power that is being shared. Appearing to share power would vitiate the simulation. Real sharing on something of importance permits whatever benefits are to be derived by all parties. The greatest risk comes from the expectations for power sharing running ahead of the instructor's intentions as revealed in the Class Council Charter. Having given an inch, why not a mile? In a later running of this simulation with undergraduates, this exposure increased, especially since the less mature students adjusted more slowly to the nuances of meaning among solo decision power, codetermination, and consultation. The adjustment is itself the learning, but in the meantime the pressure on the instructor can build and the student skepticism can slip to cynicism. "If you seek my advice and don't decide as I advise, you don't sincerely want my advice."

The set-up, administration, and debriefing of the simulation all take precious time, incremental time for the instructor. The design of the simulation front loads most of the activity early in the semester. By design as well, the elected representatives have greater access to learning directly—something which can be mitigated by careful use of these resources in the debriefing. Student risk appears to be the lock-in feature of learning of this "re-structured" class after there may be consequences for withdrawal. It's possible that international students from cultures with rigid hierarchic relationships between instructor and student would find the simulation a difficult adjustment along with all the other adjustments a guest student must make in the U.S. One final risk for the instructor is hard to avoid. There may be invidious comparisons made in other courses where power sharing is not the norm. In a similar vein, the student grapevine may contaminate expectations in later semesters. I found that prospective students knew about the power sharing and novel grading system. Discovery learning with the simulation proved difficult in successive semesters. Incidently, Prince John had difficulty slipping back into the role of benevolent dictator.

Even with all the risks, the rewards weighed heavier. I was able to get down to the levels of knowledge, attitude and skill that I wanted, despite the slippery "participation" concept across the cultures involved. Students gave clear evidence of both content and process learning. They learned about representation and learned to represent. Learning took place at all three levels identified by Serrie (1992): personal, interpersonal, and institutional. Achievement of the learning objectives was clearly enhanced by the increased accountability via ownership. Greater student interest led to greater motivation to learn. This flies in the face of Bartomome's (1988) gulag experience, probably because I was not struggling with the "chameleon" behavior in my own newly-defined instructor role. I had permanently changed colors. One unintended consequence was the closing of distance between myself and the students. After a long stint as dean and having reached the *troisième* age, I disliked the distance former status and current age tended to build between students and myself. Going from a benevolent dictatorship to a constitutional monarchy closed that distance in ways I would have not predicted.

NOTES

1. Of course there is no such thing as "European" in this context, as the E.U. has found out in attempting to legislate its own social agenda which included an employee participation plank. For our purposes, European "participation" will mean continental European, especially central and north Europe members of the E.U. These countries have enough cultural variation among themselves without complicating the story with Latin and Anglo European countries. In the expanding E.U., most observers estimate that what we here call European "participation" will shape whatever consensus eventually emerges. In most scenarios, the cultural center of gravity of the new Europe shifts northeast from Brussels.

2. In the class described here, the 35 students who met for two hours and forty minutes in each of 15 weeks came from eight countries (Colombia, India, Italy, Netherlands, Thailand, Turkey, United Kingdom, and the U.S.), with 10 foreign nationals. The group included 24 women and 11 men, 23 part-time students and 12 full-time students.

REFERENCES

Bartomome, F. (1988). Contingency Theories of Leadership and the Teaching of Organizational Behavior: A Case in Point. *The Organizational Behavior Teaching Review*, XII(4), 59-62.

Bowditch, J. and Buono, A. (1994). *A Primer on Organizational Behavior*, New York: Wiley.

Calori, R. and Dufour, B. (1995). Management European Style. *Academy of Management Executive*, IX(3), 61-73.

Ewing, D. (1981). A Bill of Rights for Employees. *Across the Board*, March, 42-49.

Ford, R. and Fottler, M. (1995). Empowerment: A Matter of Degree. *Academy of Management Executive*, IX(3), 21-31.

Gunz, H. (1995). Realism and Learning in Management Simulations. *Journal of Management Education*, XIX(1), 54-74.

Kolb, D. (1985). *Experiential Learning*, New York: Prentice-Hall.

Kolvenbach, W. and Hanau, P. (1987). *Handbook on European Employee Co-Management*, Deventer/Netherlands: Kluwer.

Levinson, C. (1974). *Industry's Democratic Revolution*, London: George Allen and Unwin.

Little, L. (1990). Beyond Role Play: Character Immersion in Organizational Behavior Class. *Organizational Behavior Teaching Review*, XIV(4), 46-53.

Mills, T. (1978). Europe's Industrial Democracy: An American Response. *Harvard Business Review*, November-December, 143-152.

O'Connell, J. (1984). Corporate Governance: The European Challenge. In Hoffman, W. et al., *Corporate Governance and Institutionalizing Ethics*, Lexington: Lexington Books, 49-54.

Poole, M. (1986). Participation Through Representation: A Review of Constraints and Conflicting Pressures. In Stern, R. and McCarthy, S., *The Organizational Practice of Democracy,* New York: Wiley, 235-256.

Sashkin, M. (1984). Participative Management Is an Ethical Imperative. *Organization Dynamics,* Spring, 4-22.

Serrie, H. (1992). Teaching Cross Cultural Management Skills. *Journal of Teaching in International Business,* III(3), 75-91.

Tannenbaum, A. (1986). Controversies About Control and Democracy in Organizations. In Stern, R. and McCarthy, S., *The Organizational Practice of Democracy,* New York: Wiley, 279-303.

Walck, C. (1992). Educating for Cultural Awareness: How Business Schools and Firms Can Share the Task of Preparing Internationally Effective Managers. *Journal of Teaching in International Business,* V(1), 31-48.

EXHIBIT A

CLASS COUNCIL CHARTER

1. Membership
   1.1 Four students.
   1.2 Three of whom must be current IB/MG 661 students.
   1.3 One may be from among the officers of the Graduate Student Association.

2. Nomination and Election
   2.1 Each of six constituent groups may nominate one candidate: female/male students, non-U.S. nationals/U.S. nationals, full-time/part-time students.
   2.2 Each student has one ballot for recording four names.
   2.3 The ballot will be written and secret.
   2.4 The top four vote receivers will be elected Council members for the semester.
   2.5 Ties are broken by those who are clearly elected, coopting the final member(s) from those who were tied.
   2.6 A four-way tie means that the ballot is null and must be repeated.
   2.7 The tellers are the last two names of non-candidates in the alpha list of family names in the class.
   2.8 The Council Chairperson will be elected by a 75% vote of the Council.
   2.9 If four ballots of the Council fail to elect the Chairperson, the instructor will appoint same.

3. Recall
    3.1 Twenty-five percent of the class may petition a recall of one or all Council members by written and signed petition.
    3.2 The secret recall ballot requires a two-thirds vote.
    3.3 If successful, the recall ballot leads to a repeat of the above nomination and election procedures.

4. Council By-Laws
    4.1 Decisions will be by majority vote.
    4.2 The Chairperson has a deciding vote in case of a tie.

5. Council Competence
    5.1 The Council decides:
        5.1.1 the policy on the number, timing, and length of breaks during class.
        5.1.2 the membership of 4 to 5 person buzz groups, whether the buzz groups should change after a time, and the composition of later buzz groups.
        5.1.3 on whether there will be produced (with resources provided by the instructor) a directory of class names, addresses and phone numbers.
    5.2 The Council co-determines with the instructor:
        5.2.1 the bases for student evaluation, considering some mix of exam, written assignment, written case analysis, paper, project, class participation.
        5.2.2 the format to be used in each: individual, pairs, groups; in-class, take-home; open-book, closed-book; instructor judgment, peer judgment.
        5.2.3 the relative weight each evaluation basis has in the final course grade.
        5.2.4 and changes in the Class Council Charter.
    5.3 The Council will be consulted on:
        5.3.1 petitions for exceptions to announced evaluation procedures, e.g., late paper, make-up exam, incomplete grade, etc.
        5.3.2 substantial alteration of the announced syllabus.
        5.3.3 rescheduling classes cancelled by weather or illness.
    5.4 The Council will be informed through the Chairperson about:
        5.4.1 any changes to the announced syllabus.
        5.4.2 the statistical distribution of grades on each evaluation basis.

6. Council Member Rights and Duties
    6.1 Rights

6.1.1 Council may call for a meeting of all students during class time, provided the instructor is given a one week's notice.

6.1.2 Council itself may meet during class time.

6.1.3 Any Council member who feels the evaluation of his or her class performance has been unfairly affected by his or her behavior as a Council Member may petition binding arbitration by a panel of four persons: two non-IB/MG 661 students selected by the Graduate Student Association officers and two persons selected by the Dean of the Graduate School.

6.2 Duties

6.2.1 Council members will respect College and Graduate School policies in their decisions.

6.2.2 Council members will honor the instructor's expressed wish for secrecy.

7. Reserved Rights

7.1 Decisions not expressly covered in this Charter are reserved to the instructor.

8. Dispute Resolution

8.1 Questions of interpretation or application of the Council Charter–if unresolved between the Council and the instructor–may be brought for binding arbitration to Attorney. . . . telephone:. . . .

EXHIBIT B

INSPIRATION FOR CLASS COUNCIL CHARTER
FROM EUROPEAN LAW

In general, the articles of the Class Council Charter (Exhibit A) have been drawn from participation legislation in Germany and the Netherlands. I have depended on a European legal source which cites the legal texts in English as well as provides commentary (Kolvenbach and Hanau, 1987). The heart of the Charter appears in article 5 "Council Competence." The Dutch Works Council Act of 1979 (ibid., Netherlands: 8) sets the basic structure in specifying the "Rights and Duties of the Works Council" under the titles "Information Rights, Advisory Rights, and Co-Decision Rights." A similar structure appears in the German legislation within the content areas of social matters, staff matters, and financial matters (ibid., Germany: 70). In our Class Council Charter we add one additional competence, that of sole decision authority (5.1) which was inspired by French legislation (ibid., France: 34) which empowers the comites d'entreprise with direct administration of certain social funds.

Beyond these most important competence matters, the Class Council Charter utilizes further European participation legislation, as in the following examples:

- the eligibility for nomination of non-class members (article 1) comes from the German board legislation which permits the election of union officials, non-employees, as employee representatives on the supervisory boards of large industrial companies (ibid., Germany: 38).
- the election procedures (article 2) reflect the common pattern of works council legislation in its care to honor various constituencies, as in Germany (ibid., Germany: 61) or Denmark (ibid., Denmark: 43).
- the Council Chairperson's tie-breaking vote (in effect, a double vote) is inspired by the powers given the chairman of the German supervisory board (ibid., Germany: 117).
- the Council's ability to commit instructor-provided resources in producing the class directory comes from the Dutch provisions which even permit the hiring of consultants at employer expense (ibid., Netherlands: 26).
- appeal to external authorities for dispute resolution (6.1.3 and 8.1) commonly appears in works council legislation, particularly in protecting the members in the performance of their duties (ibid., Netherlands: 28).
- the members' duty to honor secrecy requests of the instructor is anchored in similar provisions in Dutch law, for instance (ibid., Netherlands: 27).

EXHIBIT C

EVALUATION SYSTEM CO-DETERMINED BY THE COUNCIL AND INSTRUCTOR

TO: IB/MG 661 Students
FROM: Class Council and the instructor
DATE: 25 September
SUBJECT: Minutes of the meeting of 16 September

I. EVALUATION SYSTEM CO-DETERMINED BY THE COUNCIL AND INSTRUCTOR
   A. Directions:
      1. Each student will be evaluated on the three bases below.
      2. Each student will assign weights (within the specified ranges) to each of the bases so that the total sums to 100.

      3. Each student will submit her/his signed contract form no later than 16 October.

  B. Evaluation Bases:

      1. Mid-term exam: Done individually in take-home format. Assigned 9 October. Due 23 October. Students are welcome to discuss the exam with classmates. Expectation: more than 5 double-spaced, typed pages of text would probably be too much. Specific questions will be asked in an assignment based on the case of the day. Weight range: 20-40.

      2. Paper: Done by one or up to four students. Due 18 December. Expectation: more than 10 double-spaced, typed pages of text would probably be too much for one individual. More than 30 pages of text for the largest group would probably be too much. The topic of the paper must be agreed by the instructor and must permit independent library research. Weight range: 30-50.

      3. Class participation: 80% as judged by the instructor and 20% as judged by one's peers. Each person will be graded by each other student on the 4.0 scale, with no grade lower than 2.5. Based on the relative value of the student's contributions in class to our achieving the objectives announced in the syllabus. Weight range: 20-40.

II. OTHER DECISIONS MADE BY THE FOUR MEMBER COUNCIL

  A. Class Directory: instructor will produce a class directory of names, addresses, and day and evening phones after giving each student veto over personal information to be included.

  B. Breaks During Class Time: the instructor will provide a 10 minute break beginning within 10 minutes of 6 p.m., if possible. Until such time as the dedicated resource group members have coordinated their activities, the instructor will attempt to leave 10 minutes at the end of class for group meetings.

  C. Buzz Groups: the buzz groups will be composed of about 5 persons sitting in close proximity at the beginning of class. These groups which have begun to operate in the third class will continue to operate for a month, at which time the Council will re-examine the question.

Changing Institutional Norms and Behavior, Not Culture:
Experiential Learning Comes to Myanmar

Robert W. Hornaday

SUMMARY. This paper describes two "From-To" frameworks incorporating suggested institutional and behavioral changes that introduce experiential learning in a developing country without arousing cultural disputes. The setting is Myanmar, a country struggling to join the global economy despite severe political and economic troubles. These frameworks may be useful for those assisting MBA program start-ups in other developing countries. *[Article copies available for a fee from The Haworth Document Delivery Service: 1-800-342-9678. E-mail address: getinfo@haworth.com]*

Then, a golden mystery upheaved itself on the horizon–a beautiful, winking wonder that blazed in the Sun, of a shape that was neither Muslim dome nor Hindu temple spire. It stood upon a great knoll . . . "There's the old Shwedagon," said my companion. The golden

---

Robert W. Hornaday currently serves as Associate Professor of Management at The University of North Carolina at Charlotte.

An earlier version of this paper was presented to the Experiential Exercises and Pedagogy Track Association for Business Simulation and Experiential Learning, 1996 Meeting, in Orlando.

[Haworth co-indexing entry note]: "Changing Institutional Norms and Behavior, Not Culture: Experiential Learning Comes to Myanmar." Hornaday, Robert W. Co-published simultaneously in *Journal of Teaching in International Business* (International Business Press, an imprint of The Haworth Press, Inc.) Vol. 8, No. 4, 1997, pp. 39-48; and: *Business Simulations, Games and Experiential Learning in International Business Education* (ed: Joseph Wolfe, and J. Bernard Keys) International Business Press, an imprint of The Haworth Press, Inc., 1997, pp. 39-48. Single or multiple copies of this article are available for a fee from The Haworth Document Delivery Service [1-800-342-9678, 9:00 a.m. - 5:00 p.m. (EST). E-mail address: getinfo@haworth.com].

39

dome said "This is BURMA, and it will be quite unlike any land you know about." (quoted in *Angelene*, 1995)

–Rudyard Kipling, 1898

Kipling's observation holds true today. The Shwe Dagon pagoda still casts a golden glow over Yangon, the capital of Myanmar. (Kipling called the city and the country by their British names–"Rangoon" and "Burma.") Beneath the 2,500-year-old pagoda, modern Myanmar struggles to convert to a market system so that its people can join the global economy.

BACKGROUND

Rich in natural and agricultural resources, Myanmar was once the wealthiest country in Southeast Asia and the world's largest rice exporter. During the last days of British colonial rule before World War II, most writers believed that Myanmar had the highest literacy rate of any nation between Suez and Japan (Steinberg, p. 20). The country is bisected by the Irawaddy River system which provides a rich source of hydroelectric power, water for irrigation, and over 1000 miles of inland navigation from the Indian Ocean on the south to the Chinese border on the north.

Knowing this background, one would think that Myanmar would be reporting economic development and growth to match its fast growing neighbors in Southeast Asia such as Thailand, Malaysia, and Indonesia. Nothing could be further from the truth. In 1987, the United Nations General Assembly classified Myanmar as a "least developed nation" along with Chad, Ethiopia, Nepal, and Bangladesh (Steinberg, p. 20).

The main reason for Myanmar's economic malaise is political. The multi-party governmental system adopted after independence from the British in 1947 could not maintain internal order nor sustain economic development. Finally, in 1962, the army took direct control under General Ne Win who remained a virtual dictator for 25 years. Ne Win declared that Myanmar would follow a strange mixture of European-style socialism and populist isolationism that appealed to the xenophobic strain among the Burmese peasants.

The most striking aspect of this "Burmese Way to Socialism" was the nearly complete isolation from the rest of the world. Ne Win abruptly canceled foreign aid projects, including international exchange agreements such as the Fulbright program. Tourism was severely curtailed and citizens of Myanmar had great difficulty getting permission to travel abroad for any reason. Ne Win built a wall around Myanmar.

A description of the political and economic turmoil these policies produced is beyond the scope of this paper. Suffice to say, economic conditions in Myanmar got worse, not better (Thien, 1995). The standard of living of most people was below that of the pre-war colonial period. Black markets proliferated and influential individuals became wealthy amid wide-spread economic decline and poverty (Country Commercial Guide . . ., 1995).

In 1988, serious civil disturbances broke out. Police were unable to restore order. Regular army units, fresh from border combat with insurgent groups, shot down hundreds (perhaps thousands) in several major urban areas. Ne Win stepped down and a group of generals staged a coup. Ruling through the State Law and Order Restoration Committee (SLORC), the army leaders promised elections in 1990.

Aung San Suu Kyi, daughter of Aung San, Myanmar's martyred revolutionary hero, happened to be in Yangon during this time attending her dying mother. She became the major opposition leader and was placed under house arrest during the election campaign. Nevertheless, the opposition coalition defeated the government (army) party in the 1990 election. SLORC, however, refused to turn over power and continues (in 1995) to govern Myanmar, promising elections after a new constitution is ratified. Aung San Suu Kyi continued under house arrest for six years, becoming an international hero and winning the Nobel Peace Prize in 1991. She was released in July, 1995.

After the 1988 riots, foreign governments began to abandon aid projects in Myanmar. The suppression of dissident groups and the inability or unwillingness of the Myanmar government to control the opium trade on the Thai border led to the departure of most foreign donors including the Asian Development Bank, the United States Agency for International Development (USAID), and Japanese aid agencies. The United States withdrew its ambassador. Private foreign companies, while not forbidden to do business with Myanmar, received no assistance from governmental sources such as the World Bank, the International Monetary Fund, or the U.S. Export Import Bank. The departure of foreign donors was a major blow. Myanmar was more isolated than ever. (The previous three paragraphs digest information obtained from U.S. Embassy sources and press reports in 1995.)

Recognizing the economic reasons behind the 1988 disturbances, SLORC abandoned the command economy of the Burmese Way to Socialism and moved towards a market economy. The government eased visa restrictions on those entering and leaving Myanmar (Shin, 1995). Regulations were changed to encourage foreign investment, including provisions for foreign ownership of Myanmar corporations (Kyaw, 1995). No doubt many of these reforms were aimed at encouraging foreign donors to return, but most observers in 1995 agree that SLORC is sincere in its desire to open up Myanmar's economy. Fostering economic growth without further bloodshed is the major task faced by Myanmar's leaders.

MANAGEMENT EDUCATION NEEDS IN MYANMAR

Assuming that Myanmar can avoid a major political upheaval, the nation will require a new cadre of professional managers. The new managers will need the skills and determination necessary to meet the demands of a global market economy.

To produce these managers, universities in Myanmar must quickly create business schools that can offer Master of Business Administration (MBA) level training. This is a daunting task. The formidable obstacles faced by educational reformers include the following problems:

1. Critical funding shortages. Myanmar higher education has been cut off from the outside world since 1962. Creating MBA programs will require close contact with foreign institutions for faculty training, teaching materials, textbooks, and curriculum development. Professorial salaries are extremely low and must be raised. All this will require substantial funding. Foreign exchange is scarce in Myanmar, even for government programs.
2. Turmoil in the universities. In the wake of the 1988 troubles, the government closed the universities for four years. To accommodate students who could not enroll during the shutdown, universities began enrolling double classes in 1994. This process should be completed in 1996. Nevertheless, the overload placed a tremendous strain on university resources.

THE INSTITUTE OF ECONOMICS MBA PROGRAM

Graduate business education is big business. Around the world, MBA programs have blossomed (The Official Guide . . ., 1995). Most of the top-quality programs use English as the language of instruction. The emerging economies of Southeast Asia have been especially fertile ground. Hong Kong, Taiwan, Philippines, Malaysia, Singapore, Thailand, and Indonesia all have institutions offering English-language MBA programs. Myanmar is entering the MBA education race very late.

Notwithstanding these difficulties, the MBA Program at the Institute of Economics (IE) in Yangon welcomed its first class of 50 students in June 1995. Yi Yi Myint, the MBA Director, received an MBA from Stanford in 1960. She has based her curricula on the U.S. MBA model using English as the language of instruction. The first MBA class is a notable group. Most are young (25-30). Seventy-six percent come from the private sector, and 34% are women. Their English language capability ranges from good to excellent. Many have managed to travel outside Myanmar, so they have seen the global economy firsthand.

Yi Yi Myint formulated the following objectives and goals for the MBA Program:

Strategic Objective

> The strategic objective of the IE MBA Program is to produce graduates who have professional skills, a modern approach to management and the behavioral norms necessary to enable Myanmar to compete successfully in the world market.

Strategic Goal

> The main goal of the IE MBA Program is to develop and maintain a high quality general management Master of Business Administration program that will attract the best students in Myanmar. The IE MBA Program will seek students with well-balanced records of academic achievement, English language skills, and managerial experience.

The MBA faculty and staff moved into a converted dormitory, installed computers and air conditioners, and remodeled classrooms while classes were in session.

In June 1995, the author began a six-week assignment as an academic specialist sponsored by the United States Information Service at the U.S. Embassy in Yangon. Relations between the U.S. and Myanmar were still strained. The U.S. ambassador had not returned. The top U.S. official was the Chargé. The author's role was to assist the MBA Program by teaching classes using the case method, introducing experiential methods to junior faculty, and assisting long range planning.

From the outset, it was important that the problem of cultural issues be addressed. The author had previous experience assisting fledgling Indonesian MBA programs, and was sensitive to worries of Asian educators that business education will introduce alien, Western cultural standards that downgrade local customs and traditions.

To illustrate why these worries exist, a brief sketch of some of the characteristics of Myanmar society that become immediately apparent to a Western visitor will be helpful at this point.

SOME MYANMAR TRADITIONS AND CUSTOMS

Tradition is strong in Myanmar. Protecting traditional practices from the encroachment of Western culture is a major concern. Satellite television arrived in 1994 from India carrying "decadent" Western-style programming and exacerbating the worries of traditionalists.

Historically, Myanmar reacted strongly against cultural encroachment, especially British colonialism. Unlike other countries in Southeast Asia, Western clothing is not favored. Both sexes wear the *longyi* (a plaid sarong) and simple sandals that look like shower shoes. This attire is most striking among men who wear the longyi even on formal occasions. Trousers are seen only on soldiers and policemen, and perhaps an occasional student wearing blue jeans.

Most people in Myanmar follow the teachings of Theravada Buddhism. The unique Myanmar form of Buddhism is enriched by belief in 37 primary *nats* or spirits, a remnant of pre-Buddhist animism. Nat worship fills approximately the same role as prayers and gifts to the Saints in Christianity. Achieving *Nirvana*, or nothingness, is the major goal of Buddhist teaching. After Nirvana an individual is free from the cycle of birth, suffering, and death. To achieve this state, each must lead a life of merit.

In Myanmar, much religious activity centers around meritorious acts such as feeding monks, the constructing of Buddhist shrines and donating money for the maintenance of pagodas. People are quite business-like about merit-seeking. When a donation is made at a pagoda, the donor will often ring a bell to alert the local nats (spirits) that a meritorious act has occurred. Money donations are sometimes announced over a loudspeaker with the name of the donor and the amount of the gift.

But this does not mean that Myanmar Buddhism casts gloom over its adherents. Unlike other Asian societies, in Myanmar recounting one's achievements is not considered to be bragging or bad manners. One of the best ways of improving one's *Karma* (fate, luck) and chances for a better life next time is to rejoice in other people's successes and generosity. How can you do this if they don't tell you? No one should be shy about telling of their accomplishments. Myanmar people enjoy sharing the happiness of others.

Turning to power relationships, Myanmar has a strong tradition of centralized rule. From the earliest kings through the British colonialists, power resided in one individual, radiating down through levels of authority. Power, political or economic, has always been personal in Myanmar. Loyalty is to the person, not the office or the institution (Steinberg, p. 2). Government service is considered a major source of employment among the elite. Ne Win's methods of maintaining personal control of Myanmar for over 25 years are often compared to tactics used by the kings of old Burma (Maung, 1992).

To be successful, the new crop of Myanmar managers must be able to reconcile modern business methods with traditional Myanmar customs. Training managers who can do this is the task facing MBA programs in all developing economies.

FOCUSING ON INSTITUTIONAL NORMS AND BEHAVIOR, NOT CULTURE

The introduction of experiential learning methods, such as the case method and classroom simulations, raises the problem of alien cultural standards. Many faculty members in developing countries are hesitant to depart from traditional instructional techniques for fear of downgrading local customs and social mores. These concerns can be alleviated by focusing on institutional norms and organizational behaviors, avoiding the deeper feelings stirred by the term "culture."

Two "From-To" frameworks incorporating suggested institutional and behavioral changes provided a way to introduce experiential learning without arousing cultural disputes.

The first framework dealt with institutional behaviors—how organizations are organized and controlled (Exhibit 1). Myanmar's new breed of managers must be able to create and manage new organizations, quickly identify marketing opportunities, develop new products and services, and attract foreign capital. In addition, Myanmar's managers will have to administer the day-to-day activities of their companies, prepare strategic plans, and design organizational structure and control systems appropriate for Myanmar. To accomplish these tasks, new managers must adopt new approaches to management. The list of new approaches in Exhibit 1 is not exhaustive, but provides a good framework for discussion.

Exhibit 2 suggests some changes in managerial behavior. Increased emphasis will be placed on personal accountability, initiative, and a sense of urgency about producing high quality goods and services that can meet international competition. As Peter Drucker points out, these are not cultural changes for Myanmar, but rather behavioral changes within the Myanmar culture (Drucker, 1991). Again the suggested changes in behavioral

EXHIBIT 1. Some New Institutional Norms for Myanmar

	FROM:	TO:
Most Valued Managerial Skill	Government Relations and Technical Expertise	General Management Skills Needed to Plan, Organize, Direct and Control a Modern Business
Scope of Middle Management Interest	Functional Specialty	Complete Organizational System
Information Systems	Closed: User Must "Pull" Information from the System	Open: System "Pushes" Information to User
Focus of Efforts	Individual Success	Organizational Success
Authority Structure	Centralized	Decentralized
Competitive Scope	Local	Global

EXHIBIT 2. Some Prospective Changes in Managerial Behavioral Norms

	FROM:	TO:
Primary Organizational Goal as Seen by Employees	Provide Employment	Satisfy Customer Needs and Wants
Basis of Reward System	Loyalty	Competence
Managerial Style	Paternalistic	Self-Reliance
Individual Locus of Control	External	Internal
Path to Success	Individual Relationships	Managerial Performance

norms for Myanmar professional managers is not intended to be all inclusive, but, rather, a starting point for discussion and a way to avoid fears of cultural encroachment.

(Both Exhibits 1 and 2 were inspired by tables found in Austin, 1990, p. 233, and Beamish et al., 1994, pp. 165-178.)

RESULTS

The frameworks in Exhibits 1 and 2 provided an introduction to the discussion of the types of changes needed for economic growth in Myanmar and how experiential techniques could be used in the classroom to encourage these changes. Junior faculty became enthusiastic supporters. Although limited by the lack of teaching materials, plans are under way to write cases on Myanmar organizations and to develop classroom activities, such as in-box exercises, that are relevant.

Student response to the case method was overwhelming. Classroom interest and enthusiasm was particularly high when the author used cases he had written dealing with Indonesian companies. The Myanmar students felt a much closer affinity to the problems faced by Indonesian managers as opposed to the American cases they find in their textbooks.

CONCLUSION

The success of the MBA Program is crucial to Myanmar's economic future. Most of its neighbors in Southeast Asia are experiencing high rates of economic growth. Eager to reap the benefits of international trade, these governments are attempting to reorient their economic and political systems to attract foreign capital and to find foreign markets for their goods. Myanmar must play catch-up. Hopefully, by emphasizing changes in institutional norms and managerial behavior instead of fighting culture wars, the people of Myanmar will be able to earn their fair share of the world's economic wealth.

These frameworks may be useful for those assisting MBA program start-ups in other developing countries.

REFERENCES

Angelene, Naw. (1995) "Tourism Development in Myanmar, Visit Myanmar Year, Hotel and Tourism Infrastructure." Paper presented during the visit to Myanmar of the MBA Business Study Mission from Nanyang Technological University, Singapore.

Aung, Htin. (1995) "Human Resources Management." Paper presented during the visit to Myanmar of the MBA Business Study Mission from Nanyang Technological University, Singapore.

_____ (1995) "Country Commercial Guide: Burma (Myanmar)." Rangoon, Burma: U.S. Embassy.

Austin, James E. (1990) *Managing in Developing Countries.* New York: The Free Press.

Beamish, Paul W.; Killing, J. Peter; Lecraw, Donald J.; & Morrison, Allen J. (1994) *International Management: Text and Cases.* Burr Ridge, Ill.: Irwin.

Drucker, Peter F. (1991) "Don't Change Corporate Culture–Use It!" *The Wall Street Journal*, March 28, 1991, p. A18.

Kyaw, Myat. (1995) "The Myanmar Banking and Financial System: Public and Private Banks." Paper presented during the visit to Myanmar of the MBA Business Study Mission from Nanyang Technological University, Singapore.

Maung, Mya. (1992) *Totalitarianism in Burma: Prospects for Economic Development*. New York: Paragon House.

Myint, Myo. (1995) "Myanmar in Southeast Asia: Historical and Cultural Perspective." Paper presented during the visit to Myanmar of the MBA Business Study Mission from Nanyang Technological University, Singapore.

Shin, Tun. (1995) "Corporate and Commercial Laws of Myanmar." Paper presented seminar during the visit to Myanmar of the MBA Business Study Mission from Nanyang Technological University, Singapore.

Steinberg, David I. (1990) *The Future of Burma: Crisis and Choice in Myanmar*. Lanham, Md.: University Press of America.

Thien, Myat. (1995) "Socio-Economic and Cultural Background of Myanmar." Paper presented during the visit to Myanmar of the MBA Business Study Mission from Nanyang Technological University, Singapore.

_____ (1995) *The Official Guide to MBA Programs*. Princeton, N.J.: Graduate Admission Council.

Building Hexaflexagons Overseas:
An Experiential Exercise in Coping
with Cultural Differences

Rebecca J. Morris

M/O

J/5

C 9o

519

SUMMARY. Multicultural aspects of management are increasingly integrated into the business curricula as colleges and universities respond to the recognized need for a workforce that has a broad appreciation for the issues faced by managers in a multicultural setting, whether abroad or at home. This exercise is designed to provide students with an interesting and fun way to experience some of the frustrations encountered by managers in overseas assignments while also providing a "safe" environment for their experimentation with coping strategies.

Participants are assigned one of three roles. Participants taking the first role serve as "international experts" hired by a foreign government to train its people in the manufacture of a much valued product called a Hexaflexagon (Joint Council on Economic Education, 1992). A second group of participants play the role of the citizens of Copernia, an intensely private and collectivist society with cultural customs and taboos that are unknown to outsiders. The third group of participants serve as anthropologists conducting research on the customs of the Copernians. Difficulties in coping with cultural differences are revealed as the international experts attempt to train the

Rebecca J. Morris is Assistant Professor, Management Department, College of Business Administration, University of Nebraska at Omaha, Omaha, NE 68182.

A workshop session based on this exercise was presented by the author at the Organization Behavior Teaching Conference '94 in Windsor, Ontario.

[Haworth co-indexing entry note]: "Building Hexaflexagons Overseas: An Experiential Exercise in Coping with Cultural Differences." Morris, Rebecca J. Co-published simultaneously in *Journal of Teaching in International Business* (International Business Press, an imprint of The Haworth Press, Inc.) Vol. 8, No. 4, 1997, pp. 49-64; and: *Business Simulations, Games and Experiential Learning in International Business Education* (ed: Joseph Wolfe, and J. Bernard Keys) International Business Press, an imprint of The Haworth Press, Inc., 1997, pp. 49-64. Single or multiple copies of this article are available for a fee from The Haworth Document Delivery Service [1-800-342-9678, 9:00 a.m. - 5:00 p.m. (EST). E-mail address: getinfo@haworth.com].

Copernians in the construction of Hexaflexagons. Because the exercise involves a mythical culture and hypothetical training task, it can be effectively utilized to develop sensitivity to cultural differences in a variety of instructional settings.

Suggestions for effective use of the exercise, responses to frequently asked questions and complete directions for conducting the exercise are provided. *[Article copies available for a fee from The Haworth Document Delivery Service: 1-800-342-9678. E-mail address: getinfo@ haworth.com]*

INTRODUCTION

What happens when international experts are sent to a foreign country to train the locals to build hexaflexagons? This experiential exercise, based on a session conducted in training expatriate employees for major corporations (Hagerty, 1993), provides participants with practice in coping with cultural differences in overseas assignments. Students (especially those who have not traveled) find the exercise to be an effective experience in appreciating some of the difficulties encountered by managers in overseas assignments. They not only learn about cultural differences, but *feel* them through their participation in the exercise. In the past, many managers and also students acquired international expertise *in situ* through their international assignments or travels. However, extensive travel opportunities are not typically available to most students.

Although many different teaching approaches can be effective in pursuing an increased international emphasis, traditional lectures, discussions and case studies may yield students who are knowledgeable about theoretical similarities and differences in management concepts in a variety of cultural settings with no real experience or appreciation of the difficulties that arise in the application of those concepts. The primary objective of this experiential exercise was to provide students with an interesting and fun way to experience some of the frustrations encountered by managers in overseas assignments while also providing a "safe" environment for their experimentation with coping strategies. More specifically, the exercise has the following learning objectives:

1. *To provide students with an opportunity to explore some of the difficulties of international business through a task-related exercise.* Unlike other experiential exercises that use a non-business setting, this exercise requires students to conduct a manufacturing training session for workers from a different culture. Students respond well to

the "realism" of the exercise and have little difficulty transferring the lessons learned to a business context.

2. *To provide students with an opportunity to experience an international business interaction from "the other side."* Because the exercise involves students playing the roles of workers from a different culture, they develop an appreciation for the often unintended consequences of an ethnocentric approach to international relationships. After completing the exercise, students display a much greater understanding and sensitivity to the impact their actions and speech may have on the feelings of others.

3. *To demonstrate the importance of training and cultural preparation to the success of international ventures.* A central part of this exercise is that students in the expert role are ignorant of many of the cultural customs and beliefs of the people they are to train. Their lack of knowledge of even basic cultural customs serves as a hindrance to the accomplishment of any productive work. Students completing the exercise recognize the importance of advance cultural preparations to the selection and implementation of an appropriate training strategy.

4. *To demonstrate appropriate and inappropriate coping strategies for dealing with cultural differences in a work setting.* Past experience in conducting the exercise with either faculty or students in the expert role has demonstrated the power of the exercise to elicit many unintentional examples of inappropriate coping strategies (some of which will be discussed in subsequent sections of this paper). In debriefing, the leader can point out these inappropriate approaches and suggest more appropriate methods. Because students in the trainee roles can discuss how they felt when these inappropriate strategies were utilized, the exercise provides a powerful demonstration of the unintended impact of ethnocentric approaches.

This exercise has been successfully conducted in international management classes with graduate and undergraduate students. It has also been conducted with faculty members from a variety of disciplines at two teaching-related conferences. Although it was designed to simulate a business training session, its application may be much broader than originally intended. One participant in the exercise has utilized it in diversity workshops for nursing students. Fine Arts faculty have invited the author to conduct the exercise as part of a cross-cultural survey of art course, thus suggesting its applicability to a variety of different settings and participants.

OVERVIEW OF THE ACTIVITY

In this exercise, participants are assigned one of three roles. The first role is filled by a small group of participants who serve as "international experts" hired by a foreign government to train its people in the manufacture of a much valued product symbolized for the exercise as a paper model called a Hexaflexagon (Joint Council on Economic Education, 1992). A second group of participants play the role of the citizens of Copernia, an intensely private and collectivist society with cultural customs and taboos that are unknown to outsiders. The third group of students serve as anthropologists conducting research on the customs of the Copernians. Difficulties in coping with cultural differences are revealed as the international experts attempt to train the Copernians in the construction of Hexaflexagons. The exercise provides students with an opportunity to not only develop an appreciation for cultural differences but to actively experience them. Because the exercise involves a mythical culture and hypothetical training task, it can be effectively utilized to develop sensitivity to cultural differences in a variety of instructional settings.

SUGGESTIONS FOR EFFECTIVE USE

If the exercise is to be used in a course setting, it may be positioned early in the term for maximum benefit. Because the exercise presents a shared experience for students, it can be useful in establishing working relationships between class members. In a culturally diverse student group, the exercise effectively opens the door for comparative cultural discussions between students, thus removing barriers to cooperative learning. Early use of the exercise before topics such as cultural differences in training or the work environment are covered generally results in more unintended but negative behaviors. The exercise is memorable enough that it can effectively be utilized as an example when these topics are covered later in the term. Similarly, if the exercise is to be used in a seminar setting, it may be used as an "ice-breaker" activity to acquaint participants with one another and to start the flow of conversation.

RESPONSES TO FREQUENTLY ASKED QUESTIONS

How Realistic Is This Scenario–The implication is generally that the experts' lack of knowledge about the Copernians could not possibly happen in a "real" business situation because corporations have staff who brief managers before they leave for assignments or conduct some sort of training session. Experts often feel they would have had access to more complete information about the Copernians in the real world. This can be countered by explaining that research has shown that for U.S. firms, only 13% conduct predeparture orientation programs (Feldman, 1989). Other researchers found that 50 to 60% of U.S. firms doing international business do not conduct any cultural preparation programs (McEnery & Des Harnais, 1990). It is not unrealistic then for the experts to be unfamiliar as to aspects of the Copernian's culture. Furthermore, this issue provides the exercise leader with an excellent opportunity to discuss lack of training as a contributing factor in the higher expatriate failure rate experienced by U.S. firms (Tung, 1987).

How Realistic Are the Copernians' Customs—Although care was taken in selecting the Copernians' customs to avoid insensitive stereotypes, many of the customs are derived from actual cultural practices in different countries. Participants with previous travel experience can generally attest that the customs, though unusual, are not that far-fetched.

If the Copernians Understood English, Why the Mix-Up with Yes and No—The Copernians are instructed to express disagreement by nodding their heads vigorously and by saying "Yes." Agreement is expressed by shaking their heads and saying "No." The switching of these verbal and nonverbal symbols and their typical meanings is the source of most of the miscommunication difficulties in the exercise. Participants sometimes question the validity of this switch. One way to counter this is to provide examples of English words used in one part of the world vs. their use in other parts of the world (see Klein, 1995, for example). Once again, participants that have traveled to another English-speaking part of the world can often provide examples of being able to speak the same language, but not understand what has been communicated. Using fingers to signify the number "two" serves as an example of cultural differences in the interpretation of a nonverbal cue. In the United States, a request for two of something is often signaled by holding the index and middle finger aloft in the "V for victory" mode. In many European countries (such as France, Germany and Italy), this same symbol rewards the requester with three of the desired item since for them, the thumb counts as the number one (the number two is shown with the thumb and index finger). Difference in the traditional interpretation of verbal and nonverbal communication mechanisms also adds to the realism of the exercise because Copernians often have to stop and think before responding to a question. This simulates the communication process that might be experienced by someone for whom English is not the native language.

THE DEBRIEFING PROCESS

It is best that debriefing be done immediately following the exercise while impressions and feelings are still fresh in the participants' minds. Suggested discussion questions are provided in the appendix. During debriefing, the anthropologists should be asked to provide specific examples from their notes to support the comments of either the Copernians or the experts.

Typically, the expert's ignorance of the cultural customs of the Copernians is a severe impediment to the accomplishment of any productive training. Experts also seldom ask the Copernians to explain their behavior, believing this to be an unacceptable breach of business etiquette. Surprisingly, even the faculty members (who might be expected to have some experience in coping with a diverse student population) are unable to get past some of the basic cultural differences to accomplish the task. Both faculty and student experts exhibit behavior that might be considered offensive by the Copernians. Some experts make disparaging remarks about the Copernians in their presence, erroneously believing that they are unable to understand the English language. Others treat the Copernians as small children, carefully explaining even the most basic of instructions very slowly and in a loud voice.

At the conclusion of the debriefing, the leader should stress the importance of sensitivity to cultural differences and suggest appropriate ways in which participants could find out about cultural differences if thrust into a similar situation. Participants should be provided with examples of positive approaches to asking Copernians for help in understanding cultural differences without appearing condescending. Participants should be encouraged to view cultural differences as neither right nor wrong, just different. When approached with humility and respect, most individuals are more than willing to explain their own cultural customs to outsiders and appreciate the "experts'" willingness to learn something about their way of doing things.

REACTION TO THE EXPERIENCE

Students and faculty members that have participated in the exercise have expressed a strong positive reaction to the experience. Comments from undergraduate students indicate that the Hexaflexagon exercise is very helpful in increasing their sensitivity to cultural differences. Several students reported successfully using some of the suggestions presented in the debriefing to explore cultural differences with foreign students. Students who served as "experts" commented that while they found the experience to be frustrating, they felt more confident in dealing with future multicultural experiences as a result of what they had learned.

Faculty participants were surprised at the power of the exercise to elicit a strong response. One participant (a faculty member) became so frustrated with the Copernians' lack of progress that he noisily withdrew from the exercise, occupying a corner of the room for the remainder of the session. Because the exercise can result in such powerful emotional responses, the leader must be prepared to desensitize the situation during debriefing. Faculty that have tried the exercise in their classes or in seminars have indicated that it provided participants with a valuable experience in managing in a multicultural environment.

The importance of this type of an experience for students and managers in the 1990s is demonstrated in the following quote: "It is now generally recognized that culturally insensitive attitudes and behaviors stemming from ignorance or from misguided beliefs ('my way is best,' or 'what works at home will work here') not only are inappropriate but often cause international business failure" (Dowling, Schuler & Welch, 1994: 13). An awareness of cultural differences is critical for success in a multicultural environment. This exercise has been proven to be an effective way to provide participants with an opportunity to not only learn about cultural differences but to *experience* them in a meaningful yet fun way.

If you have any questions about conducting the exercise or wish to share your experiences, please contact the author via E-mail (MORRIS@ CWIS.UNOMAHA.EDU).

REFERENCES

Dowling, P.J., Schuler, R.S. & Welch, D.E. (1994). *International Dimensions of Human Resource Management*. Belmont, CA: Wadsworth Publishing.
Feldman, D. (1989). Relocation Practices, *Personnel*, 66(1), pp. 22-25.
Hagerty, B. (1993, June 14). Trainers Help Expatriate Employees Build Bridges to Different Cultures, *The Wall Street Journal*, pp. B1, B6.
Joint Council on Economic Education. (1992). *Work, Human Resources, and Choices* (Teachers Resource Manual). New York: Author.
Klein, G.D. (1995). Introducing the Largely Landlocked to Cross-Cultural Difference, *Journal of Management Education*, 19(1), pp. 114-122.
McEnery, J. & Des Harnais, G. (1990). Culture Shock, *Training and Development Journal*, 44(4), pp. 43-47.
Tung, R.L. (1987). Expatriate Assignments: Enhancing Success and Minimizing Failure, *Academy of Management Executive*, 1(2), pp. 117-126.

APPENDIX

BUILDING HEXAFLEXAGONS OVERSEAS:
AN EXPERIENTIAL EXERCISE IN COPING
WITH CULTURAL DIFFERENCES

OBJECTIVES:

1. To provide students with an opportunity to explore some of the difficulties of international business through a task-related exercise.
2. To provide students with an opportunity to experience an international business interaction from "the other side."
3. To demonstrate the importance of training and cultural preparation to the success of international ventures.
4. To demonstrate appropriate and inappropriate coping strategies for dealing with cultural differences in a work setting.

TIME REQUIRED: The exercise and debriefing can comfortably be completed in 1 hour and 15 minutes. Suggestions for completing the exercise in less time are provided in the directions.

NUMBER OF STUDENTS REQUIRED: Minimum of 6 students, Maximum of 40-50 students.

ADVANCED PREPARATION: The following materials are needed for this exercise:

> For each Copernian: Pencil, ruler, scissors, glue or glue stick, letter-sized paper (paper with different colored front & backside simplify the construction of the Hexaflexagons), Pattern for Hexaflexagon (A cardboard equilateral triangle with 4 inch sides. Draw a straight line across one of the points 2 inches from the bottom. Print the letter "T" in the apex of the smaller triangle formed by the line.), copy of Copernian instructions
>
> NOTE: All of the above except the instructions should be given to the international experts. Experts should not see the Copernian instructions until the end of the exercise.

> For each international expert: Copy of expert instructions, copy of Hexaflexagons, Inc. instructions, sample Hexaflexagon, materials for Copernians (listed above)

For each anthropologist: Copy of anthropologist instructions, copy of Copernian instructions, note paper and pen or pencil

NOTE: To complete the exercise in less time, select the international experts one class period in advance and distribute their directions to them. Suggest that they practice making a Hexaflexagon before coming to class. This should save approximately 10 minutes. Another way to reduce the time required to complete the exercise is to postpone the debriefing for the next class period. If this is done, it is useful to have participants jot down their reactions and impressions before leaving so that they can refer to these notes in the debriefing.

INSTRUCTIONS FOR CONDUCTING THE EXERCISE:

ASSIGNMENT OF ROLES: One anthropologist and one international expert should be selected for every 5-6 individuals in the group. In selecting the international experts, the exercise leader should be sure to include both males and females. It is also helpful to include one or more individuals with outgoing personalities as international experts. Copernians should include both males and females to permit the full impact of the exercise to be realized. The effectiveness of the exercise is determined in part by how well the Copernians play their roles, so try to select individuals who are enthusiastic about role playing. Anthropologists will primarily be observing the exercise. Gender is not an important factor in selecting anthropologists (although you may wish to include both males and females to be sure that you will obtain the full range of perceptions).

CONDUCTING THE EXERCISE: Introduce the exercise by explaining the purpose of the exercise and its foundation as a corporate training exercise reported in *The Wall Street Journal* (most students feel less foolish about the role play once they know this). Select participants for the three roles according to the guidelines in the previous section. Distribute materials as described to each participant. **IMPORTANT!** Experts must not see the directions for Copernians. Experts should leave the main room to practice Hexaflexagon construction and to develop a training strategy.

While the experts are gone, the leader should go over the Copernian instructions with the remaining participants. Copernians should be led in their practice of responses to verbal and nonverbal communications. It is important that they understand the gender based taboos and that they discuss how they will react if these taboos are violated. They should also practice their responses to yes/no questions. It is also useful to allow the Copernians to rearrange the room in a way they feel is consistent with their newly adopted culture.

While the Copernians are practicing their roles, anthropologists should be briefed on their role. Anthropologists are important in the debriefing once the exercise is completed. It is important that they take notes on verbal and nonverbal behaviors they observe. The more accurately they record their observations, the more effective the debriefing. Alternatively, the exercise could be videotaped for review by all participants—however, the presence of the camera may make participants too self-conscious to fully participate in the role play.

The leader should periodically check on the experts to make sure they understand the instructions for building the hexaflexagons. The final folding and gluing step is typically the most difficult for them. After they have constructed a Hexaflexagon (usually about 15 minutes), they may return to the room. The leader should introduce them as experts from Hexaflexagon, Inc. and allow the Copernians to proceed from there (they may wish to welcome the experts with a traditional Copernian greeting, etc.). The leader should offer only minimal assistance to either Copernians or experts during the training session. Sufficient time (at least 20 minutes) should be allowed to permit the experts to adjust their training approach as they learn more about the culture of the Copernians. If the experts become very frustrated, the leader may offer them a 5 minute recess in another room to regroup. The exercise ends once the Copernians construct Hexaflexagons (this rarely happens) or when the experts are not making much headway in accomplishing the training task.

DEBRIEFING: It is best to conduct a debriefing session immediately following the exercise, so the duration of the exercise may be timed to permit a 10-15 minute debriefing session during the allotted time. The leader may need to desensitize a particularly moving exercise by pointing out that the experts were given an extremely difficult task made much more difficult by the excellent role playing of the Copernians. Many experts will be personally disappointed with their performance during the exercise, so the leader should remind students of the need to provide positive as well as negative comments in a constructive manner. It is also helpful to reassure experts by discussing any of the leader's personal experiences with miscommunications in a multicultural setting.

The objective in the debriefing is to have students recognize the negative but unintended impact of their communications and to suggest positive ways in which these barriers can be overcome. The leader should ask students to provide suggestions of sincere, nonjudgmental ways in which the experts could have uncovered some of the problematic miscommunications.

DISCUSSION QUESTIONS: The following questions might be used in a debriefing session:

1. From the perspective of the experts: How did they feel as they conducted the training session? What was their impression of the Copernians? What were the biggest hurdles to accomplishing their task?
2. From the perspective of the Copernians: How did they feel as they participated in the training session? What was their perception of the experts? What were the biggest hurdles to overcome?
3. If the experts had to do it over again, what would they have done differently?
4. What type of information would have been useful to the experts before coming to Copernia? What would be the best method of communicating that information?
5. What could the experts have done to learn more about the Copernian's customs once the training session began?

RELATED REFERENCES:

Copeland, L. & Griggs, L. (1985). *Going International: How To Make Friends And Deal Effectively In The Global Marketplace.* New York: Plume.

Hagerty, B. (1993, June 14). Trainers Help Expatriate Employees Build Bridges To Different Cultures. *The Wall Street Journal*, pp. B1, B6.

Hodgetts, R.M. & Luthans, F. (1994). *International Management.* New York: McGraw-Hill.

Zacur, S.R. & Randolph, W.A. (1993). Traveling To Foreign Cultures: An Exercise In Developing Awareness Of Cultural Diversity. *Journal of Management Education*, 17 (4), 510-516.

EXERCISE MATERIALS

DIRECTIONS FOR INTERNATIONAL EXPERTS:

You are a member of an international engineering firm with considerable expertise in the design and construction of Hexaflexagons (a sample is attached). You have been hired by the government of the country of Copernia to train the Copernians to construct Hexaflexagons using modern and efficient manufacturing techniques.

Hexaflexagons are constructed using simple tools: a ruler, a triangle template, a pencil and scissors. Special paper is used to provide for a more colorful product. The paper also simplifies the final assembly steps of the Hexaflexagon. An instruction sheet, tools and other materials are provided for your use.

Your company has not been able to obtain reliable information about the customs and business protocols of the Copernians. You have been able to determine that most Copernians have a limited ability to speak English although few if any Copernians are able to read English characters.

Your job is to become an "expert" in the construction of Hexaflexagons (you should try it yourself to make sure you know how!). As a team, you should decide what approach you will use in training the Copernians.

You will have approximately 15 minutes to practice producing Hexaflexagons and plan your training methods before being invited into Copernia. Once in Copernia, you will have 35 minutes to conduct your training session.

DIRECTIONS FOR COPERNIANS:

You are citizens of a country called Copernia. Your country has been closed off to foreigners for many years. Only recently have tourists and business persons been permitted to enter Copernia.

Your culture loves a product called a Hexaflexagon (sample attached) but does not know how to build them. The government of your country has selected you to become part of the first group of Hexaflexagon manufacturers in Copernia. This is an important position and you are very proud to be selected. The government has also engaged a team of international experts in the design and manufacturing of Hexaflexagons to advise you on manufacturing techniques for the product. They will be arriving in 15 minutes to begin this business relationship.

Copernia has many important customs that must be followed in a business or social setting. Copernians are very demonstrative people. Greetings are exchanged by patting one another on the top of the head. Holding out a hand to someone means "Please go away." If Copernians disagree with someone, they express their disagreement by saying "Yes" and nodding their heads vigorously. It is considered impolite to conduct important business while seated. Group harmony is prized and all Copernians wish to blend in with members of their group. Any signs of independent behavior are considered a result of improper upbringing.

Perhaps most importantly, there are certain taboos in the Copernian culture. Women must never use a paper and scissors in the presence of men. Men must never use a pencil or a ruler in front of women. These taboos are central to the Copernian religion. Any break with these traditions will result in the loss of a person's status in society.

As a closed society, the Copernians have not had much exposure to other cultures. Anything different from Copernian traditions is considered foreign and suspect. Most Copernians have limited English language capabilities, but do not wish to call attention to themselves by demonstrating their abilities publicly. Few Copernians have been trained to read the English language.

Your responsibility as a Copernian is to adopt these cultural traditions and to follow them as closely as possible. The more enthusiasm you bring to this task, the more effective the exercise will be. Have fun with this!

DIRECTIONS FOR ANTHROPOLOGISTS:

You are a senior professor of Anthropology at a major university. You are intrigued by the Copernian culture and have received a research grant to travel to Copernia. Your interest is in the interaction of the Copernian culture with Westerners. You have been invited by the Copernian government to observe a historic meeting between a group of international experts and a team of specially selected Copernians.

Your responsibility is to observe the verbal and nonverbal behaviors of both the experts and the Copernians during this encounter. Take notes of specific statements, gestures, facial expressions, etc., that you observe during the interaction.

You are to remain neutral during the interaction. You will not be identified to the experts. Your sense of professional ethics requires you to refrain from any participation in the encounter. You may not serve as a translator or interpreter for fear of contaminating your research.

Hexaflexagons, Inc.*

A hexaflexagon is a hand puzzle that flips and twists. It is a good prized by people around the world. They can play with it by themselves or invent games with it to play with another person. Your firm is renowned as international experts in the construction of Hexaflexagons.

Distribute to each trainee the paper for a hexaflexagon, *Patterns for Hexaflexagon*, a ruler, and a pencil (if they do not have one). Use any training technique you desire to demonstrate and/or train the participants in the production of hexaflexagons.

During your preparation time, you should follow the directions below to prepare a sample to be sure that you master the techniques before training others. You should also decide on your strategy for conducting the training situation.

- **Step 1** Measure a strip of paper 1 1/2 inches wide and 11 inches long. (If trainees do not know how to use a ruler, demonstrate how to read the markings.)

- **Step 2** Cut out the strip.

- **Step 3** Place the strip so that the longest part goes from left to right (not up and down). Put your triangle at the left side of the strip with the "T" point at the top of the paper. Line up the base of your triangle with the bottom of the strip. Trace the outline of the triangle onto the paper. When you have created the first triangle, move your pattern over to create a second triangle beside it. Your first triangle will be right side up, the second upside down, and so on. (See the Illustration below; you may need to draw the illustration on the chalkboard.) Your triangle pattern is creating 60-degree angles. Make 10 triangles. Draw the triangles lightly with your pencil so you can erase them if you need to. (It is not necessary that students understand the concept of angles; they only need to draw the triangles.)

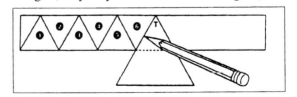

---

*These directions are adapted from *Work, Human Resources, and Choices* (Teachers Resource Manual), 1992, published by the Joint Council on Economic Education.

• **Step 4**   When your triangles are correct, retrace them with your pencil. This time press hard to score (that is, make a crease in) the paper so the lines will be easier to fold.

• **Step 5**   Cut off the excess paper at both ends so that your strip begins and ends with slanted triangle lines.

• **Step 6**   Fold the 10 triangles on the strip back and forth on the scored lines to crease the lines, placing the first triangle up, the second down, and so on. You will end up with the triangles "stacked" on top of each other. (Show students how to fold the triangles following this illustration.)

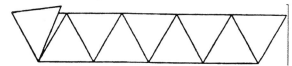

• **Step 7**   Flatten out the strip. Lightly number the triangles starting with 1 and ending with 10. Turn over and number the opposite side, make number 1 triangle match up with the first number 1.

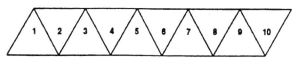

• **Step 8**   Now you are ready to fold a hexaflexagon. Hold the strip with your left hand. Fold triangle 1 to the inside (toward your right hand). Glue triangle 1 to triangle 10 of the same color. The folded piece will have six sides. (*Hex* means six.)

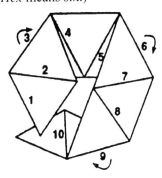

- **Step 9**   Glue together the two ends that meet, placing the first triangle over the last triangle. Flatten.

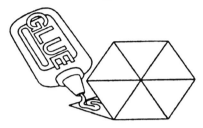

- **Step 10**   When the glue is dry, try gently twisting your hexa-flexagon on the folds until it flattens out with different sides showing.

NOTE: Larger hexaflexagons can be made if students have access to larger paper. For example, with legal-size paper the size of the hexaflexagon can be increased to 14 inches long by 2 inches wide. Use the same triangle pattern to create 10 larger triangles.

Multinational Business Gaming: Is Gender Important?

Scott D. Johnson
Denise M. Johnson
Peggy A. Golden

SUMMARY. The paper reports empirical findings of a study of students involved in international business games. Gender is introduced as a variable that may affect the individual's perception of task complexity, group cohesion, and self-confidence in the international business gaming environment. Findings suggest that females, compared with males, tend to view the simulation as less complex, have less cohesive group structures, and exhibit less self-confidence. However, game performance measures show no significant gender differences. Implications are also discussed for simulation administrators and professors using games in the context of international business training. *[Article copies available for a fee from The Haworth Document Delivery Service: 1-800-342-9678. E-mail address: getinfo@haworth.com]*

Scott D. Johnson is Assistant Professor of Marketing at the University of Louisville. Denise M. Johnson is Associate Professor of Business at the University of Louisville. Peggy A. Golden is Associate Professor of Management and International Business at Florida Atlantic University.

Address correspondence to Scott D. Johnson, PhD, Assistant Professor of Marketing, School of Business, CBPA, University of Louisville, Louisville, KY 40292.

The authors would like to express their sincere appreciation to three anonymous reviewers of this paper.

[Haworth co-indexing entry note]: "Multinational Business Gaming: Is Gender Important?" Johnson, Scott D., Denise M. Johnson, and Peggy A. Golden. Co-published simultaneously in *Journal of Teaching in International Business* (International Business Press, an imprint of The Haworth Press, Inc.) Vol. 8, No. 4, 1997, pp. 65-82; and: *Business Simulations, Games and Experiential Learning in International Business Education* (ed: Joseph Wolfe, and J. Bernard Keys) International Business Press, an imprint of The Haworth Press, Inc., 1997, pp. 65-82. Single or multiple copies of this article are available for a fee from The Haworth Document Delivery Service [1-800-342-9678, 9:00 a.m. - 5:00 p.m. (EST). E-mail address: getinfo@haworth.com].

65

International business simulations allow the student to make complex business decisions in a changing international environment, taking into consideration factors such as differential exchange rates, inflation changes, tariff fees, and other considerations typically not encountered in a domestic setting. The advanced information technology tools available today enable educators to use business simulations to help students better understand this dynamic global business environment.

As a learning tool, business simulations continue to be examined extensively. Many authors have investigated a variety of factors which impact the business simulation experience. Such studies have, for example, considered simulations as learning tools (Gentry 1980; Keys 1987; Klein 1984; Wolfe 1978), task complexity as a factor in simulation effectiveness (Cohen and Rhenman 1961; Keys 1987; Raia 1966; Wolfe 1978; Wolfe and Box 1988), the impact of group cohesiveness on team performance (Deep, Bass and Vaughan 1967; Eddy 1985; Glazer, Steckel and Winer 1987; Gosenpud, Miesing and Milton 1984; Gouran 1982; Leana 1985; McKenney and Dill 1966; Miesing and Preble 1985; Norris and Niebuhr 1980; Wolfe and Box 1988), realism as a factor in simulation effectiveness (Larreche 1987; Mehrez, Reichel and Olami 1987; Ruben and Lederman 1982; Slack 1993), the impact of leadership style and team size on performance (Gentry 1980; Rowland and Gardner 1973; Wolfe and Chacko 1983) and the types of decision processes used in simulations (Davis 1982; Hogarth and Makridakis 1981; Lant and Montgomery 1987; Muhs and Justis 1981; Ross 1987). Some studies have examined attitudes about the simulation experience (Fripp 1994; Glazer, Steckel and Winer 1987) and how attitudes affect team performance (Glazer, Steckel and Winer 1987).

An important yet neglected area of interest in the simulation literature is the role played by gender. Most of the extant research has viewed gender as being only tangentially related to larger issues. However, gender is a topic of critical importance in the area of international business, as gender differences in cultures beyond the United States are often more pronounced than those within the U.S. As more companies expand international operations, business school graduates would be well served in becoming increasingly aware of both domestic and international perceptions of gender issues.

This study examines perceptions of task complexity, group cohesiveness and self-confidence in the simulation environment, extending current research by including the role of gender and applying previously studied constructs to the international business game. Gender is discussed as a cognitive filter or schema (Malle and Horowitz 1995; Perry, Davis-Blake and Kulik 1994) that can affect group or team role behavior. By including gender as an issue, this research acknowledges that individual differences may have implications for the successful gaming experience. Also, since team performance may be expected to impact these perceptions, correlations of each of the variables with team performance are examined as well as differences with gender.

The discussion focuses first on the value of the simulated business environment. The discussion then turns to individual differences and perceptions affecting the business game. The literature is reviewed as it pertains specifically to the development of schema which might lead to gender differences in perceiving task complexity, group cohesiveness, and self-confidence. Next, the methodology of the study is described, followed by the results and a subsequent discussion of the results. Finally, implications for international business and gaming are delineated followed by a discussion of the limitations and conclusions.

THE VALUE OF THE SIMULATED BUSINESS ENVIRONMENT

Simulations have increased in popularity as a training tool among both businesses and educators. Dale and Klasson (1964) surveyed 107 AACSB schools regarding the use of simulation games. They found that 71 percent of the schools sampled were using simulation games in at least one course. Twenty-five years later, Faria (1987) reported that 95 percent of AACSB schools in his survey had faculty who used business simulation games.

In addition to the wide use of simulation games among business schools, many corporations use simulation games in their training programs (Faria 1987; Faria and Schumacher 1984; Fripp 1994; Gordon 1985; Slack 1993). Some executives note that simulations are more effective in business training since these individuals are more comfortable with "active" learning, like cases and simulations, rather than "passive" learning, like lectures and readings (Fripp 1994). In addition to the benefit of active learning, simulations allow executives to try new approaches and ideas in an environment which is safe, while receiving immediate feedback in financial terms (Fripp 1994).

Larreche (1987) noted that case studies and simulations fall between the traditional educational method of lectures/readings and the practice of actual work experience. As such, they are more action oriented than the traditional method of teaching but less risky than decision making in an actual firm. By using information from lectures and borrowing heavily from decision making, simulations provide theoretical validity from academia and behavioral validity from the business world (Larreche 1987).

Gentry (1991) noted that experiential learning is what makes simulations so popular among business educators. Virtues such as immediate feedback, realism and content orientation have also been noted by a number of other authors (Faria and Dickinson 1994; Keys, Wells and Edge 1994; Slack 1993). In addition, Faria and Dickinson (1994) noted that simulations also provide a global view, stress the interrelationship among functional variables, and allow students to gain experience without the risk of making real world wrong decisions.

INDIVIDUAL DIFFERENCES AND PERCEPTIONS AFFECTING THE BUSINESS GAME

The following section reviews the relevant literature pertaining to cognitive schema, task complexity, group cohesiveness, and self-confidence. These topics are also discussed from a gender specific focus. Additionally, the discussion links these ideas to business gaming.

Cognitive Schema

A schema is "a collection of mental representations that are interassociated and function together as a unit" (Malle and Horowitz 1995:471). The representations of the self are referred to as self-schemas. In the learning environment, schemas develop from previous learning experiences, self-esteem, cognitive preferences for certain classroom environments, and so on. In the case of gender, mental maps may develop from observations in similar situations such as on-the-job experiences (Fiske and Taylor 1984), through modification of previously held stereotypes (Holyoak and Gordon 1984), or be learned as a result of directed teaching (Perry, Davis-Blake and Kulik 1994). The research using schemas to discuss gender has generally focused on how self-schema affects perception of the individual's behavior and the behavior of others. For the purposes of this study, we look at how gender-based schemas may affect perceptions of task complexity, group cohesiveness, and self-confidence in the context of the simulated business environment.

Previous research suggests that demographic variables, as observable traits, do not explain some behavior differences in work groups (Powell 1993). However, Malle and Horowitz (1995) suggest that societally defined schemas can lead to greater probabilities of driving predictable behavior. Still other studies report differences in self-perceptions among females as it affects group decision-making and access to mentoring

(Cianni and Romberger 1995; Denton and Zeytinoglu 1993). In this context, while work teams may not openly exclude females from access to mentoring or active participation in decision-making, such exclusion is not uncommon. Thus, if socially defined schema-based differences drive behavior and gender differences exist in workplace settings and mentoring situations, it is reasonable to expect gender differences in the perception of the gaming environment.

Task Complexity

Studies examining the role of task complexity on decision-making generally agree that as perceived task complexity increases, the decision maker adopts strategies to reduce cognitive strain (Payne 1976; Olshavsky and Granbois 1979). The decision strategies, or decision heuristics, are expected to vary depending upon knowledge levels, experience, motivation, and other factors.

Several studies have examined task complexity in the simulation experience (Cohen and Rhenman 1961; Keys 1987; Raia 1966; Wolfe 1978; Wolfe and Box 1988). However, these studies have shown mixed results, finding complex games are more effective than simple games, simple games are more effective than complex games, and complex games are more realistic, more confusing and require more thinking and knowledge. Wolfe (1978) examined test scores for concepts and facts for students participating in games that were simple, moderately complex, and very complex. Although none of the differences in scores in the before simulation were significantly different from one another, total scores for both concepts and facts were significantly higher for complex games when compared with games of moderate or simple complexity. Butler, Pray and Strang (1979) found that moderately complex games produce high levels of perceived learning. In addition, researchers have suggested that learning may be more a function of individual differences among students themselves rather than the complexity of the simulation (Keys and Wolfe 1990).

Literature examining the impact of gender on perceptions of task complexity is sparse. However, there is some evidence suggesting the technology aspect of computer simulations may be viewed differently based on gender. Heinssen, Glass and Knight (1987) found that women tend to have higher levels of anxiety when using a computer, which has been traditionally perceived as a male-oriented activity (Harrison and Rainer 1992). In this context, if the task environment is less familiar, one might expect perceptions of the task environment as being more complex.

Group Cohesiveness

Group cohesiveness has been defined as a complex array of items, involving personal liking, similarities among members, a common belief in group goals, satisfaction with leadership and a shared positive group morale (Wolfe and Box 1988). Leana (1985) and Gouran (1982) found that groups with high cohesiveness tended to have higher productivity levels than groups with low cohesiveness. Norris and Niebuhr (1980) found that teams comprised of members who knew each other well prior to forming the game group did not outperform new teams; however, top performing teams developed high levels of cohesiveness over the course of the game. Miesing and Preble (1985) found similar results, where the two highest performing teams had the most group cohesiveness, and the two lowest performing teams had the least cohesiveness. However, several authors have noted that a priori cohesiveness may not necessarily affect performance in a positive manner (Deep, Bass and Vaughan 1967; Gosenpud, Miesing and Milton 1984; McKenney and Dill 1966). Nevertheless, group cohesiveness is generally expected to be linked with positive outcomes of the simulation experience.

One stream of research examining the effect of gender in group situations looks at the varying communication styles of men and women. Since women generally communicate in ways that encourage harmony and open discussion, it is believed that women excel at group work (Heim with Golant 1992; Tannen 1995). However, in a business simulation environment, this may not be the case. Business simulation games are well-known for stimulating lively discussions, with individuals often having heated arguments over decisions to be made. Given the very competitive simulation environment, an aggressive, domineering strategy may be more common than one seeking harmony. Kolb and Coolidge (1991) note that in negotiations, women tend to prefer conflict avoidance, speak less and listen more, while men tend to interrupt and openly advocate their decisions. In addition, the idea that women tend to disfavor group cohesiveness in a male-dominated situation was supported by DiTomaso, Farris and Cordero (1993).

Such behaviors may be considered to be part of gender specific socialization. Kotler (1984) notes that human behavior is largely learned. Researchers have noted that young girls, for example, often learn to play one-on-one, learn how to get along, learn how to be fair to everyone, learn how to engage in play as a process, learn how to negotiate differences, and learn how to keep the power structure completely even (Heim with Golant 1992; Tannen 1995). Young boys, in contrast, often learn that competition is a vital aspect of the game. They are taught to do what the coach says, to be a team player, to be aggressive or to appear aggressive, to take criticism and praise, to stay focused on the goal, to have a game plan, and to understand that winning is everything (Heim with Golant 1992). In this socialization context, it is not unexpected that men and women would view teamwork from different orientations. Thus, women may regard teamwork as the process of finding a win-win solution that meets everyone's needs while men may think of teamwork as following the orders within the hierarchy to achieve a goal (Heim with Golant 1992; Grymes and Stanton 1993; Tannen 1995).

Self-Confidence

Much of the business literature describes self-confidence as a characteristic possessed by effective leaders (Kirkpatrick and Locke 1991; Powell 1993). The leadership literature would lead one to believe that individuals performing well are high in self-confidence. Thus, although this concept is not yet well developed in the context of simulation research, Patz (1989) found that teams with Myers Briggs NT characteristics performed at a consistently superior level in the simulation game.

One stream of research has examined the confidence of women in communication. Findings suggest that women and men differ in their preference for patterns of speech (Kolb and Coolidge 1991; Gilligan 1982). On the whole, women tend to modify their statements with qualifiers, such as "This isn't always true" or "What do you believe is appropriate?" in order to open lines of communication for discussion. Men, on the other hand, tend to speak in more aggressive, confident terms without qualifiers. As a result, women's speech is deferential, which may be detrimental in negotiations and group work (Kolb and Coolidge 1991). McCarty (1986) and Maccoby and Jacklin (1974) note that more women than men are likely to self-report feelings of low self-confidence in task or achievement situations. This is likely to occur regardless of whether these individuals receive positive, negative, or no feedback (McCarty 1986).

The notion that women have less self-confidence is confirmed by leadership theories as well. For example, trait theories in leadership note that leaders often have certain traits or characteristics in common which are associated with male stereotypes, such as initiative, decisiveness and self-confidence (Kirkpatrick and Locke 1991; Powell 1993). In addition, behavioral theories of leadership examine those behaviors most often associated with leaders, such as dominance, control and high task-orientation (Cann and Siegfried 1990). However, it should be noted that these behaviors emphasize self-confidence based on the masculine stereotype of superiority and power (Powell 1993).

A number of studies have indicated that males are considered to have higher self-confidence since they have been socialized to develop that trait since early childhood (Grymes and Stanton 1993). Boys are often taught to win, to be more assertive, to be more independent, and to be more opportunistic than girls (Lipman-Blumen 1982; Statham 1987; Kelly 1991; Tannen 1995). Such behaviors may result in males scoring high on self-confidence measures. Furthermore, in a study examining self-confidence of students with gender, DeRosa and Wilcox (1989) found that males are significantly more confident than females.

Finally, work on masculine and feminine traits indicates that a dominance of traditional masculine traits tends to favor success in a competitive environment. Duerst-Lahti and Johnson (1989) divide a number of traits into masculine traits (predictable, task-oriented, loyal, willing to use intimidation, dominant, managerial, competitive, creative, independent, ambitious, assertive, opportunistic, risk-taking, and frank) and feminine traits (process-oriented, doing things "by the book," trusting, attractive, affectionate, emotional, and skilled in interpersonal interactions).

The studies discussed above examine factors which may directly or indirectly affect the simulation experience as a teaching or training tool in the classroom. Keys and Wolfe (1990) note that additional studies are needed to evaluate more accurately the impact of complexity and group cohesiveness on learning objectives of simulations. They also believe that group factors with regard to selection provide inconclusive results. Thus, further study on gender composition and group traits, such as self-confidence, certainly seem warranted. Finally, based on the simulation literature, there is a noticeable dearth of research effort with a focus on individual differences.

The next section provides a descriptive analysis of a student sample from two universities participating in international emphasis classes. In this study, the social dynamics and perceptions are analyzed by gender to explore decision-making differences based on this distinction.

METHODOLOGY

In order to explore these potential gender differences in the context of international business simulations, data were collected in one graduate and two undergraduate international marketing classes and two undergraduate international management classes, providing a sample consisting of 119 responses. Data were collected during the Spring and Fall semesters of 1994 and the Spring semester of 1995 after completion of simulation exercises. Teams in the simulation were self-determined. Two different simulations were utilized in these international classes, *The Multinational Management Game* (Keys, Edge and Wells 1992) and *Airline* (Smith and Golden 1995). In terms of complexity, the former is believed to offer a more complex environment to the participant (Keys 1987; Keys and Wolfe 1990).

The students were in attendance at a midwestern and southeastern urban university characterized by students that work full-time and are older (mean age = 25.67, s.d. 5.47, range 19 to 45 years old) than the population of students typically found in residential universities. Thirteen percent of the respondents were juniors, seventy-three percent were seniors and fourteen percent were MBA students. Fifty-four percent of the respondents were male, and forty-six percent were female. In the sample, the respondents did not show significant differences in age by gender (F = .97, p = .52) nor was age correlated to task complexity (r = .03, p = .72), group cohesiveness (r = .04, p = .65), or self-confidence (r = − .04, p = .67). Thus, although we cannot be certain that our sample is representative of the general population of college students, it appears that the variability in the constructs of interest is not driven by age alone. In addition, the somewhat older base of this sample may be inferred to have contributed to the development of workplace schemas.

Multi-item scales were utilized to measure each construct of interest. Nunnally (1978) notes that multi-item scales offer numerous advantages which make measures more reliable. Group cohesiveness was measured using a five-point Likert scale for each of three items, and summing the responses to each of the items. Cronbach's alpha was used to test the reliability of this scale. With an alpha value of .6767, this scale was determined to be of acceptable reliability. Task complexity was measured using three five-point Likert scales items. These three items were summed, and the Cronbach's alpha associated with this scale was .8186. Finally, self-confidence was measured using six items with six-point Likert scales. These individual items were summed, resulting in a Cronbach alpha level of .7412. The individual items and the resulting scales are described in Table 1. The task complexity and group cohesiveness items were developed for the study. Self-confidence items used in the study have appeared in other settings (Tigert 1974; Lumpkin and Hunt 1989).

RESULTS

The coefficient alphas, mean values, and standard deviations for the task complexity, group cohesiveness, and self-confidence scales are shown in Table 1. Generally speaking, students neither agreed nor dis-

TABLE 1. Scale Descriptions

Scale Items	Coefficient Alpha	Mean (Std. Dev)
Task Complexity Simulation was too complex[a,c] Simulation was easy to understand[c] I found the simulation to be difficult[a,c]	.8186	9.415 (2.851)
Group Cohesiveness I dislike working in groups[a,c] I learn a lot from other students in group projects[c]	.6767	7.691 (1.807)
Self-Confidence I am more self-confident than most people[b] I am considered a leader[b] I have never been really outstanding at anything[a,b] I am more independent than most people[b] I have a lot of personal ability[b] I often can talk others into doing something[b]	.7412	23.738 (3.665)

[a] item reverse coded
[b] six-point forced-choice Likert scale
[c] five-point Likert scale (strongly disagree to strongly agree)

agreed that the simulation was too complex (mean = 9.415). However, students did generally agree that they enjoyed working in groups (mean = 7.691). Finally, the students appeared to have relatively high levels of self-confidence (mean = 23.738).

Analysis of variance was used in order to determine whether or not any of the scales differed by gender. Scales were standardized to accommodate the differences in anchors and summed values. Level of performance, measured by asking respondents whether they were performing in the upper third, middle third, or lower third of the class, was used as a control effect, since those teams that performed well might be expected to have more favorable attitudes toward the simulation and themselves.

As can be seen in Table 2, all three scales showed significant differences with gender. Task complexity was apparently affected most by gender ($F = 9.92$, $p = .00$). None of the scales showed any effect from the performance factor. Table 2 also shows the variation in standardized mean values between males and females for each of the scales used. In all cases, the mean was lower for females than males. Thus, females tended to see the task as less complex, feel less cohesion with the group, and have lower self-confidence in the simulation context.

TABLE 2. ANOVA: Simulation Perceptions by Gender (with Performance)

	F value	p value	Female (mean)	Male (mean)
Task Complexity				
Gender	9.92	.00	− .32	.26
Perceived performance	2.37	.10		
Overall	5.39	.00		
Group Cohesiveness				
Gender	4.79	.03	− .22	.20
Perceived performance	.64	.53		
Overall	2.29	.08		
Self-Confidence				
Gender	5.06	.02	− .23	.20
Perceived performance	.31	.73		
Overall	2.06	.10		

DISCUSSION

The purpose of this quasi-experiment was to show how gender schemas may lead to differences in perceptions of task complexity, self-confidence, and group cohesiveness as they emerge in the international business gaming environment. Scores of females regarding the complexity of the task, perceived group cohesiveness, and self-confidence were lower than they were for males. Thus, an interesting finding is that while much of the complexity literature suggested females would find the simulation more complex, this was not found to be the case.

The higher perceived group cohesiveness for males may be the result of the nature of the simulation environment, where traditional masculine characteristics such as decisiveness, aggressiveness, and risk taking tend to be rewarded. Thus, the comfort males may feel from being socialized into the competitive team environment, where winning is important, may at this time exceed that of females. In this context, such characteristics may contribute positively to the schema of males and negatively to the schema of females. Females also had significantly lower scores on the self-confidence scale than males. This result is consistent with the literature in both the areas of self-confidence and decision-making. In addition, since most of the females were in groups containing one or more males, they may have felt a certain level of intimidation which has been widely noted when males and females are members of the same team (Heim with Golant 1992; Grymes and Stanton 1993; Powell 1993).

The literature suggested that differences in performance on the simulation may impact respondents' perceptions of the simulation task or environment. This was not found to be true. Thus, an interesting finding is that despite gender differences in task complexity, group cohesiveness, and self-confidence, overall self-reported performance (based on objective team ranking feedback at the end of the game) did not play a statistically significant role from a gender perspective. In fact, a frequency crosstab showed approximately equal frequencies of performance assessment by males and females.

IMPLICATIONS

Although simulations are perceived to be beneficial learning tools providing content, experience and feedback in a realistic environment (Keys and Wolfe 1990), not all participants perceive the characteristics of simulations in the same manner. In general, females may perceive simulations to be less complex than males. However, this view of the game complexity does not seem to be related to perceived performance. However, the lower self-confidence and lower perceived group cohesiveness could potentially result in team underperformance. This was not assessed in this study. In this context, the instructor or simulation administrator may want to devote some effort in building group norms before the simulation commences. The instructor might also consider testing students for those traits which tend to promote teamwork and success in a competitive environment. As a follow-up, the instructor may want to develop group training exercises prior to beginning the simulation. Males and females participating in the simulation should be aware of sex role stereotyping and how this may affect group decision-making behavior.

A key point to note is that while the traditional leadership traits often favor males, such traits do not necessarily translate into better game performance. Thus, instructors have the opportunity to point out that high performance can be achieved regardless of how one may score on traditional self-confidence measures. International business courses offer an appropriate setting to discuss culture-based gender schemas and behaviors. Thus, the idea that gender-based schemas are to a large extent learned, and may be witnessed within the simulation itself, offers a unique learning experience which can contribute to a greater appreciation of the subtleties of international business situations.

As students are trying to struggle not only with the complexities of the concepts as learned in their domestic functional classes, but also with the intricacies in the international environment, the instructor should reassure students that they should not be intimidated by the simulation, but rather embrace its nuances. This approach could be incorporated into the regular instructor guidance which has been suggested by Certo (1976), Keys (1987) and Keys and Wolfe (1990).

As academics, we must realize that we may be placing students into situations where they may be uncomfortable. It is easy to justify doing this because these students will face similar situations in the workplace. However, if we are to mimic both the positive and negative aspects of reality with the simulation, we have the responsibility to give students the tools with which to make that reality a rewarding place for all to work. We need to help students learn how these differences affect perceptions about tasks, self-confidence, and approaches to teamwork. If these students are being trained to be managers, then we should use the simulation as a vehicle to confront challenging and complex issues affecting the students themselves and the business conditions they will face.

LIMITATIONS

This particular study, while providing evidence of significant difference in perceptions between males and females, has a number of limitations. First, student samples were collected only at two public urban universities whose students are primarily part-time. Responses may vary if a larger sample is drawn from a larger group of universities. Second, a range of moderately complex simulations was used by respondents as the basis for evaluating complexity from a subjective perspective. Results may be different with tightly controlled objective levels of simulation complexity. Finally, students who have had previous contact with simulation games may find the task to be inherently less complex. However, data was not collected to measure previous exposure to the simulation experience.

Future research could examine changes in student perceptions and traits over the course of the simulation. Data collected prior to the simulation experience could measure student expectations of complexity, group cohesion, self-confidence, and performance. Measurements could be taken which could compare whether pre-simulation expectations were significantly different from post-simulation perceptions.

Additionally, how the group is formed (e.g., self-determination or assigned), how the group is organized and managed, and the specific composition of the group may affect perceptions. Do self-determined groups with a highly structured organization perform well relative to other arrangements? How do individual perceptions in all male or all female groups differ? Should teams be selected to incorporate members with certain traits?

Finally, very little research has examined the international dimension of simulations. The data reflect perceptions of students in international business classes. However, it is not clear whether the findings demonstrate perceptions specific to simulations within the international context. Thus, the issue of whether perceptions vary across types of classes is worthy of further study.

CONCLUSION

The international business simulation offers a unique opportunity to study not only complex interrelationships among functional areas of international business, but also the individual differences and perceptual factors typically linked with the socialization of people within a culture. Our female and male business graduates need experiences which will help them to be competitive in the global business environment. The international business simulation may be the perfect opportunity to open minds to cultural issues both inside and outside the gaming experience.

REFERENCES

Butler, R.J., T.F. Pray and D.R. Strang (1979) "An Extension of Wolfe's Study of Simulation Game Complexity," *Decision Sciences*, 10, 480-486.

Cann, A. and W.D. Siegfried (1990) "Gender Stereotypes and Dimensions of Effective Leader Behavior," *Sex Roles*, 23, 413-419.

Certo, S.C. (1976) "The Experiential Exercise Situation: A Comment on Instructional Role and Pedagogy Evaluation," *Academy of Management Review*, 1 (3), 113-116.

Cianni, M. and B. Romberger (1995) "Perceived Racial, Ethnic, and Gender Differences in Access to Developmental Experiences," *Group and Organization Management*, 20 (4), 440-459.

Cohen, Kalman J. and E. Rhenman (1961) "The Role of Management Games in Education and Research," *Management Science*, 7 (July), 131-166.

Dale, A.G. and C.R. Klasson (1964) "Business Gaming: A Survey of American Collegiate Schools of Business," Austin, TX: Bureau of Business Research, University of Texas.

Davis, D.L. (1982) "Are Some Cognitive Types Better Decision Makers Than Others? An Empirical Investigation," *Human Systems Management*, 3, 165-172.

Deep, S.D., B.M. Bass and J.A. Vaughan (1967) "Some Effects on Business Gaming of Previous Quasi-T Group Affiliations," *Journal of Applied Psychology*, 51, 426-431.

Denton, M. and I.U. Zeytinoglu (1993) "Perceived Participation in Decision-

Making in a University Setting: The Impact of Gender," *Industrial and Labor Relations Review*, 46 (2), 320-331.

DeRosa, DeAnna and Dennis L. Wilcox (1989) "Gaps Are Narrowing Between Female and Male Students," *Public Relations Review*, 15 (1) Spring, 80-90.

DiTomaso, Nancy, George F. Farris and Rene Cordero (1993) "Diversity in the Technical Work Force: Rethinking the Management of Scientists and Engineers," *Journal of Engineering and Technology Management*, 10 (1,2) June, 101-127.

Duerst-Lahti, Georgia and Cathy Johnson (1989) "Gender, Style and Bureaucracy: Must Women Go Native to Succeed?" Paper presented at the Annual Meeting of the American Political Science Association, Atlanta, GA (September), Figure 1.

Eddy, William B. (1985) *The Manager and the Working Group*, New York: Praeger Press.

Faria, A.J. (1987) "A Survey of the Use of Business Games in Academia and Business," *Simulation and Games*, 18 (2) June, 207-224.

Faria, A.J. and John R. Dickinson (1994) "Simulation Gaming for Sales Management Training," *Journal of Management Development*, 13 (1), 47-59.

Faria, A.J. and M. Schumacher (1984) "The Use of Decision Simulations in Management Training Programs: Current Perspectives," *Proceedings of the Association for Business Simulation and Experiential Learning*, 220-225.

Fiske, S.T. and S.E. Taylor (1984) *Social Cognition*, New York: Random House.

Fripp, John (1994) "Why Use Business Simulations?" *Executive Development*, 7 (1), 29-32.

Gentry, James B. (1991) "What Is Experiential Learning," in J.W. Gentry (ed.) *Guide to Business Gaming and Experiential Learning*, New York: Nichols/GP Publishing, 19-20.

Gentry, James W. (1980) "Group Size and Attitudes Toward the Simulation Experience," *Simulation and Games*, 11 (4) December, 451-460.

Gilligan, Carol (1982) *In a Different Voice: Psychological Theory and Women's Development*, Cambridge, MA: Harvard University Press.

Glazer, Rashi, Joel H. Steckel and Russell S. Winer (1987) "Group Process and Decision Performance in a Simulated Marketing Environment," *Journal of Business Research*, 15, 545-557.

Gordon, Jack (1985) "Games Managers Play," *Training*, 22 (7), 30-47.

Gosenpud, J.P., P. Miesing and C.J. Milton (1984) "A Research Study on Strategic Decisions in a Business Simulation," in D.M. Currie and J.W. Gentry (eds.) *Developments in Business Simulation and Experiential Exercises*, Stillwater, OK: Oklahoma State University, 161-165.

Gouran, D.S. (1982) *Making Decisions in Groups: Choices and Consequences*, Glenview, IL: Scott, Foresman.

Grymes, Sandra and Mary Stanton (1993) *Coping with the Male Ego in the Workplace*, Stamford, CT: Longmeadow Press.

Harrison, Allison W. and R. Kelly Rainer, Jr. (1992) "The Influence of Individual Differences on Skill in End-User Computing," *Journal of Management Information Systems*, 9 (1) Summer, 93-111.

Heim, Pat with Susan K. Golant (1992) *Hardball for Women: Winning at the Game of Business*, Los Angeles: Lowell House.

Heinssen, R.K., C.K. Glass and L.A. Knight (1987) "Assessing Computer Anxiety: Development and Validation of the Computer Anxiety Rating Scale," *Computers in Human Behavior*, 3, 49-59.

Hogarth, Robin M. and Spyros Makridakis (1981) "The Value of Decision Making in a Complex Environment: An Experimental Approach," *Management Science*, 27 (January), 93-107.

Holyoak, K.J. and P.C. Gordon (1984) "Information Processing and Social Cognition," in R.S. Wyler, Jr. and T.K. Skrull (eds.) *Handbook of Social Cognition*, Hillsdale, NJ: Erlbaum, 1, 39-70.

Johnson, Eric J. and J. Edward Russo (1984) "Product Familiarity and Learning New Information," *Journal of Consumer Research*, Vol. 11, June, 542-550.

Kelly, Rita Mae (1991) *The Gendered Economy*, Newbury Park, CA: Sage Publications.

Keys, J. Bernard (1987) "Total Enterprise Business Games," *Simulation and Games*, 18 (2) June, 225-241.

Keys, J. Bernard and Joseph Wolfe (1990) "The Role of Management Games and Simulations in Education and Research," *Journal of Management*, 16 (2), 307-336.

Keys, J. Bernard, Alfred G. Edge and Robert A. Wells (1992) *The Multinational Management Game*, Third Edition, Little Rock, AR: Micro Business Publications.

Keys, J. Bernard, Robert A. Wells and Alfred G. Edge (1994) "The Multinational Management Game: A Simuworld," *Journal of Management Development*, 13 (8), 26-37.

Kirkpatrick, Shelley A. and Edwin A. Locke (1991) "Leadership: Do Traits Matter?" *Academy of Management Executive*, 5 (2) May, 49-60.

Klein, Ronald D. (1984) "Adding International Business to the Core Program via the Simulation Game," *Journal of International Business Studies*, 15 (Spring/Summer), 151-159.

Kolb, Deborah M. and Gloria G. Coolidge (1991) "Her Place at the Table," *Journal of State Government*, 64 (2) April-June, 68-71.

Kotler, Philip (1984) *Marketing Management*, Englewood Cliffs, NJ: Prentice-Hall, Inc.

Lant, Theresa K. and David B. Montgomery (1987) "Learning from Strategic Success and Failure," *Journal of Business Research*, 15, 503-517.

Larreche, Jean-Claude (1987) "On Simulations in Business Education and Research," *Journal of Business Research*, 15, 559-571.

Leana, Carrie R. (1985) "A Partial Test of Janis' Group Think Model: Effects of Group Cohesiveness and Leader Behavior on Defective Decision Making," *Journal of Management*, 11, 5-17.

Lipman-Blumen, J. (1982) *Gender Roles and Power*, Englewood Cliffs, NJ: Prentice-Hall, Inc.

Lumpkin, James R. and James B. Hunt (1989) "Mobility as an Influence on

Retail Patronage Behavior of the Elderly: Testing Conventional Wisdom," *Journal of the Academy of Marketing Science*, 17, Winter, 1-12.

Maccoby, Eleanor E. and Carol Nagy Jacklin (1974) *The Psychology of Sex Differences*, Stanford, CA: Stanford University Press.

Malle, B.F. and L.M. Horowitz (1995) "The Puzzle of Negative Self-Views: An Explanation Using the Schema Concept," *Journal of Personality and Social Psychology*, 68 (3), 470-484.

McCarty, Paulette A. (1986) "Effects of Feedback on the Self-Confidence of Men and Women," *Academy of Management Journal*, 29 (4), 840-847.

McKenney, J.L. and W.R. Dill (1966) "Influences on Learning Simulation Games," *American Behavioral Scientist*, 10, 28-32.

Mehrez, Abraham, Arie Reichel and R. Olami (1987) "The Business Game versus Reality," *Simulation and Games*, 18 (4) December, 488-500.

Miesing, Paul and John F. Preble (1985) "Group Processes and Performance in a Complex Business Simulation," *Small Group Behavior*, 16, 325-338.

Muhs, William F. and Robert T. Justis (1981) "Group Choices in a Simulated Management Game," *Simulation and Games*, 12 (December), 451-465.

Norris, Dwight R. and R.E. Niebuhr (1980) "Group Variables and Gaming Success," *Simulation and Games*, 11, 301-312.

Nunnally, Jum C. (1978) *Psychometric Theory*, Second Edition, New York: McGraw-Hill Book Company.

Olshavsky, Richard W. and Donald H. Granbois (1979) "Consumer Decision Making–Fact or Fiction?" *Journal of Consumer Research*, Vol. 6, September, 93-100.

Patz, A.L. (1989) "Group Personality Composition and Total Enterprise Simulation Performance," in J. Wingender and W. Wheatley (eds.) *Developments in Business Simulation and Experiential Exercises*, Stillwater, OK: Oklahoma State University, 136-137.

Payne, John W. (1976) "Task Complexity and Contingent Processing in Decision Making: An Information Search and Protocol Analysis," *Organizational Behavior and Human Performance*, 16, 366-387.

Perry, E.L., A. Davis-Blake and C.T. Kulik (1994) "Explaining Gender-Based Selection Decisions: A Synthesis of Contextual and Cognitive Approaches. *Academy of Management Review*, 19 (4), 786-820.

Powell, Gary N. (1993) *Women and Men in Management*, Second Edition, Newbury Park, CA: Sage Publications.

Raia, Anthony P. (1966) "A Study of Education Value of Management Games," *Journal of Business*, 39, 339-352.

Ross, William T. (1987) "A Re-Examination of the Results of Hogarth and Makridakis' 'The Value of Decision Making in a Complete Environment: An Experimental Approach,'" *Management Science*, 33 (February), 288-296.

Rowland, K.M. and D.M. Gardner (1973) "The Uses of Business Gaming in Education and Laboratory Research," *Decision Sciences*, 4 (April), 268-283.

Ruben, D. and C. Lederman (1982) "Instructional Simulation Gaming: Validity, Reliability and Utility," *Simulation and Games*, 13, 233-244.

Slack, Kim (1993) "Training for the Real Thing," *Training & Development*, May, 79+.

Smith, Jerald R. and Peggy A. Golden (1995) *Airline*, Third Edition, Englewood Cliffs, NJ: Prentice-Hall, Inc.

Statham, Anne (1987) "The Gender Model Revisited: Differences in Management Styles of Men and Women," *Sex Roles*, 16 (7/8), 409-429.

Tannen, Deborah (1995) "The Power of Talk: Who Gets Heard and Why," *Harvard Business Review*, 75 (5) September-October, 138-148.

Tigert, Douglas J. (1974) "Life Style Analysis as a Basis for Media Selection," in William D. Wells (ed.) *Life Style and Psychographics*, Chicago, IL: American Marketing Association.

Wolfe, Joseph (1978) "The Effects of Game Complexity on the Acquisition of Business Policy Knowledge," *Decision Sciences*, 9, 143-155.

Wolfe, Joseph and Thomas M. Box (1988) "Team Cohesion Effects on Business Game Performance," *Simulation and Games*, 19 (1) March, 82-98.

Wolfe, Joseph and Thomas I. Chacko (1983) "Team-Size Effects on Business Game Performance and Decision-Making Behaviors," *Decision Sciences*, 14 (January), 121-133.

Index

Numbers in *italics* indicate figures; "t" following a page number indicates tabular material.

Haworth
DOCUMENT DELIVERY
SERVICE

This valuable service provides a single-article order form for any article from a Haworth journal.

- *Time Saving:* No running around from library to library to find a specific article.
- *Cost Effective:* All costs are kept down to a minimum.
- *Fast Delivery:* Choose from several options, including same-day FAX.
- *No Copyright Hassles:* You will be supplied by the original publisher.
- *Easy Payment:* Choose from several easy payment methods.

Open Accounts Welcome for . . .
- Library Interlibrary Loan Departments
- Library Network/Consortia Wishing to Provide Single-Article Services
- Indexing/Abstracting Services with Single Article Provision Services
- Document Provision Brokers and Freelance Information Service Providers

---

MAIL or *FAX* THIS ENTIRE ORDER FORM TO:

Haworth Document Delivery Service
The Haworth Press, Inc.
10 Alice Street
Binghamton, NY 13904-1580

or FAX: 1-800-895-0582
or CALL: 1-800-342-9678
9am-5pm EST

PLEASE SEND ME PHOTOCOPIES OF THE FOLLOWING SINGLE ARTICLES:

1) Journal Title: _____
   Vol/Issue/Year: _____ Starting & Ending Pages: _____
   Article Title: _____
   _____

2) Journal Title: _____
   Vol/Issue/Year: _____ Starting & Ending Pages: _____
   Article Title: _____
   _____

3) Journal Title: _____
   Vol/Issue/Year: _____ Starting & Ending Pages: _____
   Article Title: _____
   _____

4) Journal Title: _____
   Vol/Issue/Year: _____ Starting & Ending Pages: _____
   Article Title: _____
   _____

(See other side for Costs and Payment Information)

COSTS: Please figure your cost to order quality copies of an article.

1. Set-up charge per article: $8.00
   ($8.00 × number of separate articles)   _____

2. Photocopying charge for each article:
   1-10 pages: $1.00   _____

   11-19 pages: $3.00   _____

   20-29 pages: $5.00   _____

   30+ pages: $2.00/10 pages   _____

3. Flexicover (optional): $2.00/article   _____

4. Postage & Handling: US: $1.00 for the first article/
   $.50 each additional article   _____

   Federal Express: $25.00   _____

   Outside US: $2.00 for first article/
   $.50 each additional article _____

5. Same-day FAX service: $.35 per page   _____

   GRAND TOTAL: _____

METHOD OF PAYMENT: (please check one)

❑ Check enclosed   ❑ Please ship and bill. PO # _____
   (sorry we can ship and bill to bookstores only! All others must pre-pay)

❑ Charge to my credit card: ❑ Visa; ❑ MasterCard; ❑ Discover;
   ❑ American Express;

Account Number: _____ Expiration date: _____

Signature: *X* _____

Name: _____ Institution: _____

Address: _____

_____

City: _____ State: _____ Zip: _____

Phone Number: _____ FAX Number: _____

MAIL or *FAX* THIS ENTIRE ORDER FORM TO:

Haworth Document Delivery Service   **or FAX:** 1-800-895-0582
The Haworth Press, Inc.   **or CALL:** 1-800-342-9678
10 Alice Street   9am-5pm EST)
Binghamton, NY 13904-1580